AI
in
Education

★*Developments,*
★*Practical Tools,*
★*Personalized Learning Strategies,*
and
★*Ethical Considerations of*
Using Artificial Intelligence
in the Classroom

Edward Foster

Contents

Introduction

I imagine stepping into a classroom of the near future. As you approach your desk, you can almost feel the pulse of energy as artificial intelligence (AI) seamlessly integrates into the learning environment. Picture yourself as a teacher who, with the help of AI, instantly tailors lesson plans to suit each student's unique learning style and pace. Envision a world where intelligent systems efficiently manage administrative tasks, allowing educators more time to inspire and engage their students. This is not just a distant dream—it's a rapidly approaching reality, and this book is your guide to understanding and embracing it.

My name is Edward Foster, and I am deeply fascinated with the convergence of AI and education. I come from a family of educators: both my parents and no less than two of my aunts have teaching backgrounds. So did my late grandfather, a true teacher in heart and soul who was the principal of a locally renowned elementary school at the height of his career.

As for myself, one could say that I "grew up together" with AI in education: as a little boy in elementary school, I saw its cradle. When I was in high school, we both traversed the complexities of adolescence, each in our own respective ways. We found ourselves being taken slightly more seriously by the time I graduated from college, and today, both of us continue to learn and develop as full-grown adults.

Driven by a desire to make a useful contribution to education of my own by demystifying the complexities of AI for educators, I have crafted this book to bridge the gap between high-tech concepts and their practical applications in classrooms worldwide.

This book aims to make AI both accessible and actionable. Whether you're an innovative, seasoned teacher curious about AI or a future-oriented school administrator eager to improve operational efficiency, this guide will equip you with the knowledge and tools necessary to enhance teaching and learning outcomes.

Structured to flow from theory to practice, the book opens with an exploration of fundamental AI concepts, followed by practical tools and strategies for integrating AI into educational settings. Each chapter builds on the last, covering ethical considerations and preparing you for future implications of AI in education. Unlike other texts, this book emphasizes real-world applications and includes case studies and success stories to illustrate how AI is already making a difference in classrooms around the globe.

Navigating new technologies can be daunting. That's why I've designed this book to be a user-friendly companion for educators and administrators of all backgrounds. Whether you have a technical background or are new to AI, the content is crafted to be engaging, clear, and, most importantly, applicable.

Throughout your journey with this book, you will find detailed, step-by-step guides on implementing AI tools, recommendations for the best resources, and best practices proven effective in the educational sector. This book is not just about theoretical knowledge; it's about taking actionable steps toward integrating AI into your educational practices.

Prepare to take on the roles of both observer and active participant in the AI revolution in education. This introduction will serve as a gateway into the world of AI in education, carefully designed to engage, inform, and inspire you to explore and implement AI tools in your teaching and administrative tasks.

As we move forward, I invite you to keep an open mind and consider AI's endless possibilities. You are at the forefront of a significant educational transformation. Embrace this opportunity to become a pioneer in adopting AI technologies, enhancing your capabilities, and ultimately enriching your students' academic experiences.

Before we embark on this exciting journey together, I'd like to point out one more thing to you out of both honesty and diligence: I wrote this book with substantial help from AI software. I had the idea to write it and what its contents should consist of, but the writing and research were mostly conducted with help from AI.

Why? I want to show you how AI has helped me as a writer and how it will help you as a teacher or administrator.

Edward Foster

Chapter 1
Understanding AI in Education

In the bustling corridors of a modern school, the whisper of a revolution is growing louder, a transformation driven by AI that promises to reshape how we teach and learn. As educators and administrators, you stand on the brink of this educational evolution, where the integration of AI can streamline administrative tasks and unlock new and personalized ways to engage every student. This chapter aims to equip you with a solid understanding of AI's fundamental concepts, enabling you to appreciate its potential and prepare for its integration into your educational practices.

1.1 Decoding AI:
Definitions and Fundamentals for Educators

Artificial intelligence is a term that conjures up images of robots and futuristic technologies, but its implications in the educational sphere are both profound and immediate. At its core, AI involves the creation of intelligent machines that work and react like humans, learning from their environments and taking autonomous actions.

For educators, understanding AI starts with familiarizing oneself with key terminology that demystifies this field.

Machine Learning, a subset of AI, is where the magic begins. It refers to algorithms that allow computers to learn from and make data-based decisions. Algorithms can be defined as human-programmed, computerized processes that are to be followed in calculations and other problem-solving issues. Unlike traditional programming, where tasks are explicitly programmed, machine learning enables systems to learn and evolve from experience without being explicitly programmed. Think of it as teaching your students a concept and then allowing them to independently apply that knowledge to solve new problems.

Neural Networks are another cornerstone of AI. Inspired by the human brain, these networks are interconnected nodes (akin to neurons) that process information by responding to external inputs, relaying information between each node. The process involves inputs being fed into the network, which then processes them through multiple layers that extract features and patterns, ultimately leading to an output.

Natural Language Processing (NLP) allows computers to understand, interpret, and generate human language in a meaningful and helpful way. Tools like *Siri* or *Alexa*, which you might already be using to check the weather or play music, are powered by NLP. They interpret your voice commands and respond accordingly. In educational settings, NLP can be utilized to develop tools that read text, interpret language, and even gauge sentiment, making it possible to provide feedback on student essays or facilitate complex discussions in online forums.

Understanding these technologies is crucial for educators because they have the potential to enhance learning and represent a shift toward more personalized and engaging educational experiences. By automating routine tasks, AI frees up time for teachers to focus more on interactive and creative teaching methods. For instance, AI can automate the grading of multiple-choice tests and administrative tasks like attendance and scheduling, reducing the time teachers spend on paperwork and increasing the time they can dedicate to their students.

AI also holds the key to personalized learning, a pedagogical approach that tailors teaching methods, educational activities, and academic content to the needs of individual learners. For example, Machine Learning algorithms can analyze data on students' performance and learning habits, adapting instructional material to suit their unique learning speeds and styles. This maximizes individual student's learning potentials and addresses diverse learning needs in a classroom, ensuring no student is left behind.

◊ Interactive Element: AI Terminology Quiz

To reinforce your understanding of the AI terminologies discussed, try this quick multiple-choice quiz (5 questions) to test your knowledge. Answers can be found right after the final question.

1. What are algorithms?
A. Computers.
B. Robot-programmed, computerized processes that are to be followed in calculations and other problem-solving issues.
C. Human-programmed, computerized processes that are to be followed in calculations and other problem-solving issues.
D. Software like Microsoft Office.

2. Computers equipped with AI can learn from their environments and make autonomous decisions.

A. True

B. False

3. Have a look at the following two statements:

1) A cornerstone of AI, Neural Networks are not inspired by the human brain.

2) Alexa is an excellent example of a device that is powered by Natural Language Processing (NLP).

Are these statements true or false?

A. 1 is true, 2 is false.

B. 1 is false, 2 is true.

C. Both statements are true.

D. Both statements are false.

4. Name an example of an educator's task AI can automate.

A. Provide a student with emotional support.

B. Grading of multiple-choice tests.

C. Maintain order in the classroom.

D. Talk to parents to discuss a child's progress.

5. Can AI help with personalized learning?

A. Yes.

B. No.

Answers: 1C, 2A, 3B, 4B, 5A.

By grounding yourself in the fundamental concepts of AI, you are better prepared to navigate its applications in the educational sector. This knowledge empowers you to implement AI-driven tools effectively and enables you to foresee and harness their potential to transform educational environments for the better.

Today, AI is not just a tool for automating tasks but a versatile ally in the quest for more profound, meaningful education. However, one must also consider its origins and evolution to truly appreciate the breadth and depth of AI's impact on education.

1.2 The Evolution of AI in Educational Systems: A Historical Perspective

The journey of AI in education is a fascinating tale of evolution, from its nascent stages in the mid-20th century to its current status as a transformative force in classrooms around the globe. Initially conceptualized as mere machines capable of performing tasks that typically require human intelligence, AI's role in education has expanded dramatically, reshaping how educational content is delivered, consumed, and understood.

In the early days, programmed learning machines, which were rudimentary in design, introduced the educational sector to the concept of machine-assisted learning. These machines were simple devices that provided students with questions and delivered feedback based on their responses. While primitive, these early systems paved the way for developing more sophisticated educational technologies.

Let's zoom in on three essential developments on AI's timeline that occurred from the 1970s to the 1990s.

1. *Intelligent Tutoring Systems (ITS)* started to emerge. One of the earliest forms of AI in education, ITS provided feedback and personalized instructions to learners based on their performance and interactions.

2. AI techniques started to be utilized for educational purposes, whereby computers were programmed to deliver instructions and simulate educational environments. This formed the start of *Computer-Based Learning (CBL)*.

3. The incorporation of AI elements in educational software, like adaptive learning algorithms and NLP, began to be developed. These systems aimed to provide personal learning experiences and enable automation for specific academic tasks.

Even with the significance of these developments, it is only in recent decades, with advances in computational power and data availability, that AI has begun to fulfill its potential. The real turning point came with the advent of the personal computer and the Internet, facilitating a new era of digital learning tools. This period witnessed the creation of more dynamic educational software that could adapt to individual learning paces—a precursor to today's adaptive learning systems.

As we moved into the 21st century, the milestones became even more significant with the implementation of AI in more complex educational tasks. One notable development was the introduction of AI scoring systems in standardized testing. These systems could evaluate written responses to open-ended questions, providing scores and feedback that mirrored human judgment. This innovation demonstrated AI's potential to assume roles that require cognitive abilities, such as understanding text and evaluating complex student inputs.

Another significant milestone was the deployment of AI for personalized learning plans. Through the use of sophisticated algorithms, educational platforms could now analyze vast amounts of data on individual students' learning habits and preferences. This capability allowed for the creation of customized learning experiences that adapt in real time, offering each student a tailored educational journey. Programs like *DreamBox Learning*, which uses AI to adapt math teaching to the student's level, have shown significant positive effects on learning outcomes, underlining the effectiveness of AI-enhanced personalized learning.

The impact of these developments on educational methodologies and outcomes cannot be overstated. Traditional, one-size-fits-all teaching methods are being supplemented—and sometimes replaced—by AI-driven models emphasizing personalization and engagement. Teachers are now equipped with tools that allow them to meet the individual needs of each student, a task that was once daunting due to the sheer diversity of learning styles and paces in a typical classroom. Furthermore, AI has taken on the labor-intensive aspects of education, such as grading and scheduling, freeing teachers to devote more time to instructional roles and student interaction.

Educators who have embraced these changes confirm the profound impact AI has had on their professional lives and their students' learning experiences. For instance, a high school math teacher reported that integrating an AI-based assessment tool not only improved her students' test scores but also saved her countless hours in grading, allowing more time for one-on-one tutoring sessions. Another educator highlighted using an

AI-powered language learning app that provided his ESL students with real-time feedback, significantly improving their engagement and accelerating their language acquisition.

These testimonials underscore a broader trend: as AI evolves, its potential to enhance education grows. With each advancement, educators gain more powerful tools to educate and inspire their students. As we look to the future, the trajectory of AI in education points to even greater integration, where AI not only supports but actively enhances the learning process through more interactive, responsive, and personalized educational experiences. The ongoing development of AI technologies promises to continue reshaping the academic landscape, offering exciting possibilities for the next generation of learners and teachers alike.

1.3 Essential AI Technologies: An Overview for Non-Tech-Savvy Educators

For many educators, the world of artificial intelligence can seem engulfed in a fog of technical jargon and complex concepts. However, the essence of AI and its educational applications can be distilled into clear, understandable elements directly relevant to day-to-day teaching and administrative tasks. Let's simplify these complex AI technologies to see how they can be practically applied in educational settings.

One of the most impactful uses of AI in education is in the realm of grading and assessment. AI-driven systems can now take on the time-consuming task of grading assignments and exams, particularly multiple-choice and fill-in-the-blank tests. But beyond these basic tasks, AI technologies can also assess more complex responses such as essays and open-ended responses. These systems utilize advanced algorithms to analyze text for grammar, coherence, and even content relevance. For instance, AI grading tools like *Turnitin's Gradescope* allow educators to quickly provide personalized feedback and grades by learning from the grading patterns previously established by the teachers themselves. This speeds up the grading process and ensures consistency in evaluation standards.

Personalized learning is another area where AI has made significant strides. AI systems can analyze a vast array of student data—from past academic performance to engagement levels in learning activities—to tailor educational experiences to individual needs. These systems adjust the difficulty level of tasks, recommend additional resources, and even modify learning pathways in real time to suit each student's learning pace and style. For example, platforms like *Content Technologies, Inc.* use AI to create custom textbooks that match the curriculum and learning objectives specific to a class or student group, allowing for a highly personalized learning experience.

Early detection of learning disabilities is a crucial yet challenging aspect of education. AI technologies are increasingly used to identify signs of learning disabilities such as dyslexia or ADHD early in a child's educational journey. By analyzing patterns in a student's interactions with digital learning tools—such as the time taken to complete tasks, the frequency of errors, and the ability to follow instructions—AI can flag potential learning issues before they become significant obstacles. Tools like *Glean Education* use AI to provide educators with insights into students' learning patterns, enabling timely intervention tailored to each student's needs.

Moreover, for those who wish to delve deeper into AI's workings and potential applications in education, several online resources and tutorials can provide more extensive knowledge and hands-on experience. Websites like

Coursera and *edX* offer courses specifically designed for educators looking to integrate AI into their teaching practices. These platforms provide both the theoretical foundations of AI in education and practical insights into using AI tools effectively in the classroom.

By breaking down AI into its fundamental applications—grading, personalized learning, and the detection of learning disabilities—and providing easy-to-understand visual aids and resources, this technology becomes less daunting. AI's role in education can be seen not just as a technological advancement but as a practical tool that can significantly enhance educational delivery and administration. As educators become more comfortable with these technologies, the integration of AI into everyday educational practices is likely to become more widespread, ultimately leading to more efficient and effective learning environments.

1.4 Comparing AI in Education Across Different Countries

The global landscape of AI in education is as diverse as it is dynamic, reflecting a myriad of approaches shaped by distinct cultural, policy, and educational frameworks. By examining the implementation of AI in education across different countries, we can glean valuable insights into how various elements influence the adoption and success of these technologies. Nations like Singapore, Finland, and the USA, each with its unique educational ethos, offer instructive examples of how AI can enhance learning environments.

Singapore, renowned for its robust educational system and technological prowess, has embraced AI to maintain its edge in global education standards. The Singaporean government has implemented AI as a part of its

Smart Nation initiative, integrating technology into every aspect of life, including education. AI tools in Singaporean schools are used for tasks ranging from personalizing learning experiences to automating administrative processes. The cultural context here, which prizes efficiency and innovation, has made integrating AI in education broadly acceptable and supported.

Furthermore, policies such as the *ICT Masterplans* for education promote the use of technology in schools, providing clear guidelines and substantial funding to support AI initiatives. These policies facilitate the integration of AI and ensure that its implementation is aligned with the broader educational goals of enhancing learning outcomes and preparing students for a digital economy.

In contrast, Finland's student-centered approach to education focuses on how AI can support individual learning styles and foster an inclusive educational environment. Finnish educational culture highly emphasizes equality and individual learning, which translates into AI applications designed to support personalized learning and special education needs. For example, Helsinki's AI experiment involved the use of machine learning to identify students at risk of dropping out, providing early support to those in need. The Finnish government supports these initiatives through its *AI Programme*, which aims to make Finland a leader in the application of AI. This ambition extends into the field because of its strong emphasis on research and development in AI, backed by partnerships between educational institutions and tech companies. This collaborative approach ensures that AI solutions are technologically advanced and pedagogically relevant.

Across the Atlantic, the USA presents a mosaic of AI adoption in education, with its implementation varying significantly from one state to another. The decentralized nature of the American educational system allows for a wide range of AI applications influenced by local policies and cultural attitudes toward technology. In some areas, AI is used extensively to enhance personalized learning and improve educational outcomes, while in others, issues such as data privacy concerns and lack of funding hinder its adoption. Federal initiatives like the *National AI Research and Development Strategic Plan* provide a framework for AI integration. Still, the diversity of implementation across the country highlights the impact of local policies and cultural values on the adoption of new technologies in education.

Several lessons emerge from these case studies that can guide educators and policymakers in other contexts. The importance of supportive policy frameworks cannot be overstated; whether it is Singapore's government-led initiatives, Finland's focus on collaborative R&D, or the USA's strategic national plans, clear policies play a crucial role in successfully integrating AI in education. Additionally, the cultural context shapes how AI is perceived and utilized in educational settings. In countries with a strong emphasis on technological innovation and efficiency, such as Singapore, the adoption of AI in education tends to be more widespread and accepted. Conversely, in cultures with more concern about technology's implications on privacy and individuality, the adoption might be more cautious and contested.

These comparisons reveal that while AI can significantly enhance educational practices, its implementation must be carefully managed to align with local educational goals and cultural expectations. This alignment ensures that AI tools are not just adopted but are also effective in enhancing learning outcomes and operational efficiency in schools. By drawing lessons from leading nations in AI education, educators and policymakers worldwide can better navigate the complexities of integrating AI into their own educational systems, ensuring that they harness the potential of AI to enrich learning experiences while remaining sensitive to local needs and values.

1.5 AI Myths Debunked: Separating Fact from Fiction in Education with AI

The rapid integration of artificial intelligence into educational settings has sparked a wide array of opinions and myths that often cloud the genuine potential and realistic capabilities of AI in schools. It's crucial to address these myths head-on, providing clarity through fact-based insights that help educators understand what AI can and cannot do and how it should be ethically deployed in educational environments.

One of the most pervasive myths is that AI will eventually replace teachers. This notion stems from an overestimation of AI's capabilities in replicating human empathy, creativity, and the nuanced understanding necessary for effective teaching. While AI can enhance teaching by providing personalized learning paths or automating administrative tasks, it lacks the ability to fully understand human emotions and respond with the empathy that is often required in the educational process. Research in AI applications underscores that the most effective educational practices arise from a synergy between human educators and AI tools.

For instance, a study in the *"Journal of AI Research"* demonstrated that classrooms that utilized AI to handle administrative and routine instructional tasks enabled teachers to dedicate more time to student interaction and creative teaching strategies, thus enhancing the learning experience without replacing the human touch.

Another common misconception is that AI is only useful for teaching STEM (science, technology, engineering, and mathematics) subjects. This myth likely finds its roots in the initial applications of AI, which were heavily focused on areas like data analytics and logical reasoning. However, AI's role in education has expanded dramatically across various subjects, including languages, arts, and humanities. AI-powered tools are now used to help students learn languages through natural language processing applications, enhance engagement through interactive history lessons, and even support artistic creativity by suggesting modifications and improvements in real time. By debunking this myth, educators across all disciplines can explore how AI might enrich their teaching practices and curriculum offerings.

Ethical considerations are also at the forefront of discussions surrounding AI in education, especially concerning privacy and the potential biases within AI algorithms. These concerns are not unfounded, as AI systems are only as unbiased as the data they are trained on, and poor data handling can lead to invasions of privacy. It is essential, therefore, to implement AI solutions that adhere to strict data protection standards and are transparent about their data use policies. Furthermore, ongoing efforts in the AI community are focused on developing algorithms free from biases. For example, initiatives like the *AI Fairness 360* toolkit by IBM aim to help developers detect and mitigate bias in AI models.

These tools ensure that AI applications in education are equitable and just, providing all students with fair learning opportunities.

As educators navigate the realm of AI in education, they need to approach this technology with a critical mindset. Rather than accepting claims at face value, they should seek out reputable sources and empirical evidence to understand the capabilities and limitations of AI.

Questions to consider might include:

- What data does this AI application collect?

- How does the AI model ensure fairness and accuracy?

- What measures are in place to protect student privacy?

Engaging with these questions will not only allow educators to make informed decisions about integrating AI tools but will also enable them to advocate for ethical AI practices that align with educational goals and values.

By addressing these myths and providing factual corrections, we empower educators to harness AI's potential responsibly and effectively. Understanding AI's capabilities, limitations, and ethical implications allows educators to integrate this technology in ways that genuinely enhance teaching and learning rather than being swayed by misconceptions and hype. As AI's development continues to progress, so too should our understanding and application of this transformative tool in educational settings, ensuring that it serves to support and augment the educational journey rather than detract from it.

1.6 The Educator's AI Toolkit:
Essential Resources and How to Use Them

In the dynamic landscape of education, where the demand for efficiency and personalization is ever-increasing, AI tools and resources emerge as essential elements in transforming educational practices. In order to empower educators to navigate and utilize these tools effectively, it is crucial to outline a clear and accessible toolkit that categorizes these resources based on their applications, ranging from administrative tasks to enhancing student engagement and facilitating personalized learning environments.

For administrative efficiency, AI tools like *Automate.io* and *Zapier* streamline routine tasks by integrating different software applications to automate workflows. For example, attendance records can be automatically updated into spreadsheets, and notifications can be sent to students and parents without manual input. These tools significantly reduce the administrative burden on educators, freeing up more time for instructional activities and student interaction.

In the realm of personalized learning, platforms such as *Knewton* provide adaptive learning technologies that tailor educational content to the needs of individual students. By analyzing data on students' performance and learning habits, these platforms adjust the instructional material in real-time, ensuring that each student can learn at their optimal pace and level. Utilizing such tools in the classroom involves initial setup phases where student data is inputted, followed by ongoing monitoring to refine the learning algorithms based on student performance continually.

Enhancing student engagement can be effectively achieved through AI-driven gamification tools like *Classcraft*, which transform learning experiences into interactive, game-based activities. These tools make learning more engaging and incorporate rewards and feedback systems that motivate students and enhance their learning outcomes. Implementing such tools typically requires educators to integrate them into existing lesson plans and tailor the game settings to align with educational goals.

To harness these tools effectively, educators must follow a structured approach to implementation:

1. **Initial Setup**: Begin by defining the educational goals you want to achieve with the AI tool. For example, if an AI-driven gamification tool is used, the goal might be to increase student engagement in a specific subject.

2. **Integration**: Integrate the AI tool with existing educational platforms and databases. This might involve technical setup, such as software installation and data migration, which can be facilitated by IT professionals if necessary.

3. **Customization**: Customize the tool settings to meet the specific needs of your classroom. This could involve setting up personalized learning paths on an adaptive learning platform or customizing the gameplay elements in a gamification tool.

4. **Testing and Feedback**: Before full-scale implementation, conduct a pilot test of the tool in a controlled environment to gather feedback from a small group of students and make necessary adjustments.

5. **Full Implementation**: Roll out the tool to the entire class or school, providing training for other educators as necessary. Continuously monitor the tool's performance and student outcomes, making adjustments to optimize its effectiveness.

Beyond using AI tools, educators must engage in continuous learning and community engagement to stay updated on the latest AI developments and best practices. Numerous online courses and workshops are available on platforms like *Coursera*, *edX*, and *FutureLearn*, offering both introductory and advanced modules on AI in education. These learning opportunities enhance educators' technical skills and provide insights into innovative pedagogical approaches that integrate AI technologies.

Moreover, participation in online forums and educational technology communities, such as *EdSurge* or the *International Society for Technology in Education (ISTE)*, allows educators to exchange ideas, share experiences, and collaborate on projects. These communities serve as invaluable resources for educators to gain support, ask questions, and learn from peers who are also integrating AI into their teaching practices.

In embracing these AI tools and resources, educators are not just adopting new technologies but becoming part of a broader movement toward more innovative, efficient, and personalized education. By effectively implementing these tools, educators can enhance their teaching methods, better engage their students, and ultimately foster an environment where both teaching and learning are more productive and enjoyable.

The continual exploration and adoption of AI in education open up new horizons for educators and students alike, promising a future where education is not only about information delivery but about nurturing a deeper, more interactive learning experience.

Chapter 2
Practical AI Tools and Applications

Imagine a classroom where each student's learning experience is uniquely tailored to their interests, strengths, and challenges. In this environment, educators are equipped with tools that respond to each student's interactions and evolve to improve engagement and understanding continuously. This chapter delves into the transformative world of interactive AI learning environments, reshaping educational landscapes by offering personalized learning paths and enhancing the overall academic experience.

2.1 Interactive AI Learning Environments: Tools That Are Shaping the Future

In the vanguard of educational technology, platforms like *Carnegie Learning* and *Smart Sparrow* stand out as pioneers, illustrating the profound impact of AI on education. These platforms are designed to adapt dynamically to each student's interactions, making learning more engaging and personalized. For instance, Carnegie Learning employs sophisticated

AI algorithms to provide real-time feedback and tailored instruction in mathematics, adapting to students' learning speeds and styles. Similarly, Smart Sparrow is designed to create adaptive learning experiences that cater to the diversity of learner profiles in any classroom setting

Implementing these interactive AI environments requires thoughtful integration into your daily teaching routines. The first step is to familiarize yourself with the platform by exploring its features and understanding its capabilities. Next, align the tool with your educational objectives by determining the initial parameters to suit your curriculum needs. This setup involves defining the learning paths, inputting the necessary instructional content, and establishing the assessment metrics.

As you integrate these tools into your classroom, continuous monitoring is crucial. This means regularly checking the system's analytics to assess student progress and engagement levels. Based on this data, you can make informed adjustments to optimize the learning experience. Lastly, evaluating the effectiveness of these AI tools is essential. This can be done through direct feedback from students and by measuring the learning outcomes against your educational goals.

The success stories of schools that have embraced these AI-driven platforms are both inspiring and illuminating. For example, a high school in California implemented Carnegie Learning's math platform and saw a significant improvement in student test scores within a single academic year. Teachers reported that students were more engaged and that the AI's personalized feedback helped students understand their mistakes and learn more effectively. Another case involves a middle school in Australia that used Smart Sparrow to create a science curriculum that adapted to each student's learning process, improving academic performance and increasing student interest in science topics.

The scalability and accessibility of these AI learning environments are critical factors that ensure their effectiveness across different educational settings. These platforms are designed to be scalable, meaning they can be effectively used in classrooms with varying numbers of students—from small groups to large lecture halls. Moreover, their cloud-based nature ensures they are accessible to any school with an internet connection, thus overcoming geographical and physical constraints. In terms of catering to diverse learning needs, AI platforms are equipped with tools that accommodate various learning disabilities and linguistic differences, ensuring that all students, regardless of their background or learning capabilities, have access to personalized and compelling learning experiences.

◊ Interactive Element: Engagement and Achievement

Consider the potential changes in student engagement and achievement you might observe by integrating AI learning environments into your classroom. Reflect on how these tools could address your challenges in meeting diverse learning needs. Write down your thoughts and any concerns about implementing such technology. This exercise will help you critically evaluate the suitability of interactive AI tools for your teaching context and prepare you for a more informed implementation process.

By exploring the leading platforms, understanding the implementation strategies, and learning from the success stories of other institutions, you are better equipped to make decisions about integrating AI into your educational practices. AI tools revolutionize the learning experience, making education more adaptive, engaging, and inclusive. As you consider these technologies, think of them as tools and partners in your mission to educate, capable of bringing out the best in both you and your students.

2.2 AI and Personalized Learning: Tools for Customized Education Plans

In modern education, the term "personalized learning" is increasingly synonymous with integrating AI technologies designed to adapt educational content to the learning pace and style of each student. Tools like *Knewton* and *DreamBox* stand at the forefront of this innovation, utilizing advanced algorithms to analyze student data meticulously. These platforms adjust the learning paths dynamically, ensuring that each lesson is not only accessible but also challenging enough to promote substantial academic growth.

Knewton, for instance, uses an adaptive learning engine that continually processes student data to customize the delivery of educational material, making learning more responsive and tailored to individual needs. Similarly, DreamBox offers a math learning environment that intelligently adjusts to a student's responses, fostering more profound understanding and proficiency at a comfortable pace for each learner.

The benefits of such personalized learning environments are substantial. They often lead to increased student achievement, as learners are bored by content that is too easy and overwhelmed by content that is too difficult. Motivation naturally increases when students feel their learning experiences are customized and relevant, which can lead to higher engagement levels.

Speaking about customizing learning experiences and making them relevant, I remember how I, back when I was in high school, was working on probability equations in math class once. My book described the problems to be solved like this: 35 marbles in a vase. 11 are blue, 8 are green, 6 are red, and 10 are yellow. Determine the probability of randomly picking a red marble. My thoughts: how bored do you need to be to sit in front of a vase with marbles, randomly pick one, and then get excited about figuring out exactly how small or big the chance was that you picked the one you did?

Utterly deprived of motivation due to my perceived lack of relevance and with an outright aversion to mathematics, I consistently scored grades in this subject that were different from the passing kind. Had AI tools been available to me at the level they are today, there is no doubt in my mind that my math grades would nowhere near have been as ghastly as they were.

However, these advanced AI tools have their challenges. Data privacy emerges as a significant concern, as these systems rely on the continuous collection and analysis of detailed student information to function effectively. Ensuring the security of this data and maintaining the trust of students and parents is paramount. Additionally, there is the risk of over-reliance on technology, which might lead some educators to sideline the irreplaceable human elements of teaching, such as empathy, creativity, and moral guidance.

A structured approach is necessary for educators eager to implement these AI-driven personalized learning tools. Initially, clear learning objectives must be established that align with both curriculum goals and the capacities of the AI tool. Following this, educators should be trained in the technical use of the platform and in interpreting the wealth of data these tools provide. This data must be used to continually adjust and refine teaching strategies and learning materials to suit the evolving needs of students.

Feedback mechanisms are also crucial; they should be built into the learning process to allow students to reflect on their learning experiences and outcomes, providing valuable insights that can further refine the AI algorithms.

Ongoing professional development is crucial in keeping up with the rapid advancements in AI technology. Educators should be encouraged to regularly update their skills and knowledge through workshops, courses, and seminars that focus on the latest developments in AI-driven educational tools. This continuous learning approach ensures educators remain at the cutting edge of educational technology, allowing them to utilize AI tools effectively and responsibly.

As AI technologies develop, so too should the methodologies employed by educators, ensuring that they remain relevant and effective in a rapidly changing educational landscape. This proactive approach not only enhances the capabilities of educators but also ensures that students receive the most current and practical educational experiences possible. It's a win-win.

Incorporating AI into personalized learning represents a significant shift in educational methodologies that offers exciting possibilities for enhancing student learning outcomes. As these tools become more refined and their use more widespread, the academic landscape will continue to evolve, offering more personalized and effective learning experiences for all students.

2.3 Enhancing Engagement Through Gamification and AI

Gamification in education refers to the integration of game design elements into non-game contexts, a practice that leverages the inherent human desire for competition, achievement, and reward. When incorporated into educational settings, these elements transform the learning process, making it more engaging and interactive, which can lead to increased student motivation and improved retention of information.

AI-driven gamification tools such as *Classcraft* and *GradeCraft* take this concept a step further by personalizing the gaming elements based on individual student data. These platforms use AI to monitor each student's progress and adapt the game mechanics accordingly. For example, suppose a student excels in a particular area. In that case, the AI might offer them more challenging quests within the game or provide additional resources or hints if it detects areas where they are struggling. This tailored approach ensures that students receive personalized support that aligns with their individual learning paths and that the game elements engage them.

Integrating gamification into the curriculum can be a transformative strategy, but it must be done thoughtfully to ensure that it enhances educational outcomes without undermining the seriousness of learning. One best practice is to clearly define the educational objectives before introducing any game elements. Educators should determine what they aim to achieve with gamification, whether it's increasing engagement, reinforcing material, or assessing understanding, and then align the game mechanics to these goals. For example, points and leaderboards might be used to encourage competition and motivation, while badges and achievements can serve as milestones to mark progress and proficiency.

Another key practice is to ensure the inclusivity of the gamified elements. Games in education should be designed to cater to diverse learning styles and abilities. This might mean offering multiple ways to earn points or progress, ensuring that tasks are not solely competitive, and providing options that cater to different strengths and interests. Additionally, the feedback provided through these platforms should be constructive and immediate, helping students understand where they have excelled and where they need further improvement, thus supporting a continuous learning cycle.

Some educators may have reservations about incorporating gamification into their teaching despite the benefits. Concerns often revolve around the potential for gamification to distract from learning objectives or the fear that it might encourage superficial rather than deep learning. There is also the consideration of time investment, as setting up and managing gamified elements in a curriculum can be time-consuming. Addressing these concerns requires educators to balance game elements and educational content. The key is to use gamification to complement traditional teaching methods rather than replace them. Activities should be closely tied to learning objectives and designed in a way that the game mechanics reinforce the educational content rather than detract from it.

Furthermore, educators must continuously monitor the impact of gamification on student learning. This involves observing changes in engagement and achievement and soliciting feedback from students about their experiences. Such feedback can provide insights into how students perceive game elements and whether they contribute positively to the learning environment. This ongoing evaluation allows educators to adjust the gamification strategy, ensuring that it remains effective and aligned with student needs and educational standards.

When implemented strategically, gamification enhanced by AI can transform the educational experience, making learning more engaging, personalized, and fun. By carefully designing gamified elements that align with educational goals, catering to diverse learning needs, and continuously evaluating their impact, educators can effectively integrate this innovative approach into their teaching practice, thereby enriching the learning journey for their students.

2.4 AI Tools for Streamlining Administrative Tasks

In education, where the focus should ideally remain on teaching and nurturing students, administrative tasks, though necessary, can often be cumbersome and time-consuming. This is where AI tools step in to revolutionize the way educational institutions handle routine administrative functions. By integrating AI-driven technologies such as automated grading systems, attendance tracking, and scheduling assistants, schools can significantly reduce the administrative load on educators, allowing them more time to dedicate to direct student engagement and instructional duties.

Automated grading systems, for instance, utilize advanced algorithms to assess student assignments and tests quickly and consistently, thereby eliminating the need for manual grading of every single paper or test. This not only speeds up the feedback process but also ensures a level of objectivity in scoring, as the AI systems adhere strictly to the grading rubrics set by the educational institution. AI-driven attendance tracking systems streamline another time-intensive task by automatically recording student attendance as they enter the classroom. This system not only saves time at the beginning of each class but also provides accurate attendance data that educators and administrators can instantly access and analyze. Similarly,

AI scheduling assistants can manage complex timetables and resource allocations, which are often a logistical challenge in schools. These systems can optimize the use of classrooms and other facilities, handle rescheduling automatically, and even send real-time updates to students and staff about any changes, ensuring smooth operations across the campus.

Integrating these AI tools into existing school management systems and databases requires careful planning and execution to ensure seamless operation and data consistency. The first step in this integration process usually involves a detailed assessment of the current IT infrastructure and administrative processes to identify compatibility and scalability issues. Following this, AI solutions need to be customized to align with specific institutional needs and integrated with existing software systems such as *Student Information Systems (SIS)* and *Learning Management Systems (LMS)*. This integration allows for a unified platform where data flows smoothly between various applications, reducing the likelihood of errors and ensuring that all stakeholders have access to the most current and accurate information.

The impact of reducing administrative tasks through AI is profound. Educators find themselves with more time to focus on what they do best—teach, engage with students, and develop innovative educational strategies. For example, a secondary school in Oregon implemented an AI-based grading and attendance system and reported that teachers saved, on average, three hours per week, which they could redirect towards tutoring students and preparing more interactive lessons. Another school in Toronto used an AI scheduling assistant to manage its resources and facilities, resulting in a 20% increase in operational efficiency and a noticeable reduction in scheduling conflicts and classroom shortages.

These case examples underscore the significant improvements in operational efficiency and educational outcomes that can be achieved by adopting administrative AI tools. Schools can optimize their resources by automating routine tasks and creating an environment where academic and administrative efficiency coexist harmoniously. As AI technology continues to grow, so does its potential to streamline more complex administrative tasks, thus promising even more significant benefits for educational institutions worldwide. This evolution marks an essential shift in the administrative realm of education, where technology and learning operate hand in hand to foster a more effective and engaging educational experience.

2.5 Virtual and Augmented Reality in Education: More Than Just a Novelty

In today's educational landscape, *Virtual Reality (VR)* and *Augmented Reality (AR)* are more than buzzwords; they represent a significant shift in how educational content can be delivered and experienced.

VR immerses users in a completely virtual environment, typically through a headset that isolates them from the real world and presents a digitally created space where they can interact. AR, conversely, layers digital enhancements over the real world, augmenting what users see, hear, and feel without removing them from their natural environment. When applied in educational settings, these technologies offer unique opportunities to engage students in ways that traditional methods cannot match.

Platforms like *Google Expeditions* and *zSpace* are at the forefront of integrating VR and AR into educational experiences. Google Expeditions allows students to embark on virtual field trips across the globe, exploring everything from the coral reefs of the Caribbean to the surface of Mars, all from the safety and comfort of their classroom. zSpace, similarly, utilizes AR to transform standard curricular content into interactive, three-dimensional experiences, making complex subjects like human anatomy, mechanical engineering, and molecular chemistry more tangible and understandable.

These tools captivate students' imaginations and deepen their understanding by allowing them to interact with the subject matter in a hands-on, immersive manner.

If you were to ask your class whether or not they are familiar with VR and AR, odds are you would see multiple hands go up, as many students already enjoy playing computer games that use these technologies. These positive connotations might make it substantially easier to integrate VR and AR successfully into your teaching methods.

Implementing VR and AR in educational settings does require careful planning and consideration, particularly regarding the hardware involved and the management of classroom dynamics during immersive sessions. For VR, you will need headsets and compatible computers or mobile devices that can handle high-quality graphics without lag, ensuring a smooth and immersive experience. AR often requires less specialized equipment, sometimes just smartphones or tablets with AR capabilities and apps designed to overlay digital information onto the physical world. Setting up these technologies involves not just a financial investment in the hardware but also an investment in training educators to use them effectively.

Classroom management during these sessions is imperative; clear guidelines must be established to ensure that students remain focused on the educational goals of the experience. This can include structured session times, specific objectives for each session, and supervision to ensure that the use of the technology remains on track.

The educational benefits of VR and AR are supported by a growing body of research and numerous testimonials from educators who have witnessed their impact first-hand. Studies have shown that VR and AR can significantly enhance student engagement and motivation, particularly in subjects that benefit from visual representation and practical experience. For example, a study published in the *"Journal of Educational Psychology"* found that students who used VR environments for learning had higher retention rates and better understanding of complex concepts compared to those who used traditional learning resources. Furthermore, educators often report that students demonstrate a higher level of excitement and participation in lessons that incorporate VR and AR, translating to an increased enthusiasm for learning and exploration.

However, it's not just about engagement; these technologies offer unique advantages in accommodating diverse learning styles and needs. VR can provide a powerful visual context for abstract concepts. At the same time, AR can provide hands-on interaction without needing physical materials, which can be particularly beneficial in resource-limited settings. Moreover, the immersive nature of VR and the interactive quality of AR can be beneficial for students with learning disabilities, providing them with alternative ways to access and engage with content that might be less accessible through traditional formats.

Incorporating VR and AR into education represents a significant step toward a more interactive, engaging, and effective learning environment. As these technologies continue to develop and become more accessible, their potential to transform educational practices grows. For educators, staying informed about the latest developments in VR and AR, understanding the practicalities of their implementation, and recognizing their potential to enhance learning are crucial steps toward harnessing these technologies to their full potential. By doing so, educators can offer students a better education and a truly transformative learning experience.

2.6 Implementing AI Language Tools: From Translation to Literacy Improvement

In the diverse landscape of today's classrooms, where students often come from varied linguistic backgrounds, AI language tools like *Duolingo* and *Babbel* have revolutionized the way language learning is approached. These tools leverage adaptive exercises and interactive tests to provide personalized learning experiences that are engaging and incredibly effective in helping learners grasp new languages. Duolingo, for example, uses a combination of listening exercises, spoken language practice, and grammar puzzles to build competence, adjusting the difficulty based on the learner's progress. Babbel takes a more conversational approach, emphasizing practical vocabulary and real-life speaking situations to boost confidence and fluency.

Beyond facilitating language acquisition, AI tools are crucial in breaking down language barriers in multilingual classrooms, ensuring that no student feels left out due to language limitations. From personal experience, for international schools in particular, the benefits of integrating such technology would be nothing short of tremendous. AI-powered translation tools can instantly convert textbooks, exams, and other educational materials into multiple languages, making content accessible to all students regardless of their primary language. Moreover, AI-driven literacy tools are particularly transformative. They assist in teaching reading and writing by providing real-time feedback, highlighting errors, and suggesting corrections. This instant feedback is invaluable in helping students improve their literacy skills quickly and efficiently.

The implementation process involves several strategic steps for educators looking to integrate these AI language tools into their curriculum. Initially, it's important to select tools that best fit the specific needs of the students and align with the curriculum goals. Once the appropriate tools are chosen, integrating them into daily lessons can be planned. For language classes, these tools can serve as supplementary aids, offering additional practice and reinforcement of material covered in class. Translation tools can help non-native speakers better understand complex concepts and instructions in subjects like science or math. Regularly reviewing the data generated by these AI tools allows educators to track progress and identify areas where students may need more support or advanced challenges.

Addressing the ethical and cultural considerations is vital when implementing AI language tools. It's essential to ensure that these tools are used in a way that respects cultural differences and promotes inclusivity. For instance, translation tools must be accurate and sensitive to the nuances of different languages to avoid misinterpretations that could lead to confusion, miscommunications, or cultural insensitivity. Furthermore, educators must be vigilant about data privacy and the ethical use of AI, ensuring that student data is protected and used responsibly to support learning without compromising privacy.

Working on the integration of AI language tools in education requires a thoughtful and informed approach. By embracing these technologies, educators can enhance language learning and literacy, making education more accessible and equitable for all students. As AI advances, its role in education will undoubtedly expand, offering even more innovative ways to support and enhance learning across languages and cultures.

2.7 Introducing a Free AI Tool: ChatGPT

ChatGPT is an artificial intelligence language model developed by *OpenAI*. It is designed to understand and generate human-like text based on the input it receives. It belongs to the family of Generative Pre-trained Transformers (GPT), which are models trained to use large amounts of text data to predict and generate coherent sentences. This is one of the tools I used to help me write this book, but it can certainly be utilized in educational settings as well.

Key features and capabilities of ChatGPT include:

- Natural Language Understanding: It can comprehend and interpret human language input across a wide range of topics and contexts.

- Text Generation: ChatGPT can generate responses, stories, summaries, and other forms of coherent text based on the input it receives.

- Conversational Abilities: It can engage in extended conversations, maintain context over multiple exchanges, and respond appropriately to user queries and prompts.

- Contextual Awareness: The model incorporates context from previous interactions to generate more relevant and coherent responses.

- Applications: ChatGPT is used in various applications such as customer service chatbots, educational tools, creative writing assistants, and more.

◊ Interactive Element: Experiment with ChatGPT

In my opinion, the best way to really get a feel for ChatGPT is to simply try it out. So let me help you do exactly that. Using a small experiment with their free version, I will guide you through it step by step. If you're already acquainted with ChatGPT, you can skip this experiment and proceed to the next chapter.

1. Open a web browser, either on your phone or on a computer.

2. In the address bar, located at the top of your screen, type in chatgpt.com

3. Press Enter. You will now be taken directly to ChatGPT.

4. Towards the bottom of your screen, there will be a bar outlined in gray in which it says "Message ChatGPT". Click on this bar. You will notice a blinking cursor appear, meaning you can now start typing your task for ChatGPT, which is known as a prompt.

5. Let's pretend you want ChatGPT to help you explain the Pythagorean theorem to a student who isn't good at math. Type in the following prompt: *Explain the Pythagorean theorem to a student who isn't good at math. Utilize simple terms and make use of an easy, practical example.*

6. Final step: Press enter and watch how ChatGPT does the rest! With the help of the result generated, you might very well be able now to help your student understand the Pythagorean theorem.

Now, having experimented with an AI tool for an educational purpose, take a moment and think of the countless possibilities you have at your disposal to take your teaching practices to a whole new level. You may want to write some of them down.

Looking ahead, the world of AI promises even broader applications and deeper integrations into education. The next chapter will explore how these technologies are shaping the future of educational assessments and evaluations, offering insights into how AI can provide more nuanced and comprehensive analyses of student learning and progress. This exploration will not only highlight AI's transformative potential in reshaping educational practices but also emphasize the importance of strategic implementation to fully realize the benefits of this powerful technology.

Chapter 3
Strategies for AI Integration and Classroom Management

E nvision a classroom where technology is not a barrier but a bridge to more extraordinary educational achievements. In this chapter, we will explore the practical and methodical steps necessary to weave AI seamlessly into the fabric of even the most low-tech environments. The goal is to make this transition as smooth as possible, ensuring that every student benefits from the integration of AI, regardless of the starting technological baseline of their educational setting.

3.1 Step-by-Step Guide to Introducing AI in Low-Tech Classrooms

Taking the first step towards integrating AI into a classroom, especially one that might lack the latest technological advancements, can seem daunting. However, this process can be demystified with a systematic approach, and you can set up your classroom for success in the digital age.

The key lies in the following actions that are to be undertaken in the order listed:

1. A thoughtful assessment;

2. A strategic choice of tools;

3. A phased implementation plan that respects both the educators' and students' pace of adaptation;

4. Monitoring and evaluation.

Assess Current Infrastructure

Before introducing any AI tools, thoroughly assessing your classroom's existing technological infrastructure is crucial. This initial assessment should focus on hardware like computers and internet connectivity and the software and platforms currently in use. Are the computers in your classroom capable of supporting new AI software? Is the internet connection stable and fast enough to handle AI applications that require high bandwidth? Understanding these elements will help you identify necessary upgrades to support an AI-enabled learning environment. Often, the upgrades required might be minimal, such as increasing internet bandwidth or updating existing devices, which can be cost-effective compared to overhauling the entire tech setup.

Identify Appropriate AI Tools

Choosing the right AI tools is of vital importance. The tools you select should align with your educational goals and the technical capacity of your classroom. Start with AI applications known for their ease of use and minimal technical requirements. Tools like AI-based educational games or simple learning analytics platforms can be ideal starters. These tools should serve a dual purpose: enhancing the learning experience for students and providing a gentle introduction to AI for educators. Importantly, opt for AI tools that offer robust support and training materials to ensure you can troubleshoot issues and maximize the tool's potential in your teaching.

Develop a Phased Implementation Plan

Introducing AI into your classroom should be a gradual process, structured in phases that allow both educators and students to become comfortable with the new technology. Start by integrating AI tools that do not disrupt the existing curriculum but instead enhance it. For instance, you might begin by using an AI tool that assists with grading student work or offers personalized learning recommendations. As confidence and familiarity with these tools grow, you can gradually introduce more complex AI systems. This phased approach not only eases the transition but also helps identify what works best for your specific educational environment without overwhelming the users.

Monitor and Evaluate Progress

Continuous monitoring and evaluation of the impact of AI tools on teaching and learning are essential. This ongoing analysis will help you understand how effectively the AI meets educational goals and where adjustments might be needed. It also provides critical feedback that can inform future technology integrations. Tools like learning analytics platforms can offer insights into student performance and engagement, which are invaluable for evaluating the effectiveness of AI in your teaching practices. Regularly assessing the impact of AI also allows you to demonstrate the value of technology investments to stakeholders, which can be crucial for securing further funding and support.

◊ Interactive Element: Implementation Checklist

To aid in the successful integration of AI in your classroom, here is a checklist that can guide your process:

1. **Technology Assessment:** Review current hardware and internet capabilities.

2. **Goal Alignment:** Ensure AI tools align with educational objectives.

3. **Ease of Use:** Select user-friendly AI tools with strong support resources.

4. **Phased Introduction:** Gradually introduce AI tools, starting with simpler applications.

5. **Training:** Participate in training sessions and utilize available support materials.

6. **Monitoring and Feedback:** Regularly assess the impact and gather feedback from students.

By following these steps, you can effectively integrate AI technologies into your classroom, even if starting from a low-tech baseline. This strategic approach ensures that the transition is smooth and sustainable, paving the way for enhanced educational outcomes through the thoughtful use of AI.

3.2 Balancing AI and Traditional Teaching Techniques

In the evolving educational world, integrating AI offers exciting possibilities. However, it is of the essence to strike a balance, ensuring that these technologies complement rather than replace the irreplaceable human elements of teaching. AI can handle administrative duties with unmatched efficiency, freeing educators to focus on their profession's creative and interpersonal aspects. This balance emphasizes the role of the teacher not just as a conveyor of information but as a mentor, facilitator, and guide in a more interactive and engaged learning environment.

One effective strategy is to promote blended learning environments where AI tools work in concert with traditional teaching methods. Blended learning combines online digital media with traditional classroom methods, requiring the physical presence of both teacher and student while providing control over the pace, time, and place of learning. AI can personalize learning content, adapting to the needs of individual students. At the same time, traditional methods ensure that a skilled educator's nuanced understanding and human touch guide the learning journey. For instance, while an AI program can provide instant feedback on a student's quiz, a teacher can offer deeper insights into misunderstood or missed concepts. This strategy not only enhances learning outcomes but also preserves the essence of traditional teaching by fostering a human connection, critical thinking, and adaptability among students.

Incorporating AI into the classroom doesn't equal relegating traditional methods to the background. Instead, it involves creating a synergy where both approaches augment each other. For example, AI-driven data analytics can offer detailed insights into student performance, which teachers can use to tailor their instructional strategies. Conversely, traditional group discussions and hands-on projects provide rich, contextual learning experiences that AI currently cannot replicate. By integrating AI tools into these activities, teachers can enhance engagement and provide a more tailored learning experience that addresses each student's individual strengths and weaknesses.

Professional development workshops play an important role in equipping educators with the skills needed to balance AI and traditional teaching methods effectively. These workshops can demonstrate practical ways to seamlessly integrate technology into the classroom and highlight successful strategies that other educators have used. For instance, a workshop might include a session on using AI tools for routine tasks like grading and attendance, paired with strategies for using the freed-up time to engage students in more meaningful, project-based learning experiences. These training sessions are invaluable in helping educators feel more confident and competent in using technology as a complementary tool rather than a replacement for their teaching practices.

The balance between AI and traditional teaching can also be seen in classrooms that have effectively integrated technology without losing the personal touch that is critical to effective education. Take, for example, a high school in New Jersey where teachers use an AI system to monitor students' progress in mathematics. The system provides students with personalized exercises that adapt to their learning pace, while teachers use insights from the system to provide targeted help to students who are struggling. This blended approach has not only improved students' test scores but has also allowed teachers to spend more time addressing individual learning challenges, thus enhancing the overall quality of education.

With these examples, I want to show you that the key to success lies in viewing AI as a tool that enhances rather than replaces traditional teaching methods. By finding the right balance, educators can leverage the best of both worlds, combining the efficiency and personalization of AI with the irrefutable value of human interaction and creativity in teaching. This balanced approach not only makes the integration of AI into the classroom more effective but also ensures that the education provided is rich, diverse, and deeply engaging.

3.3 Classroom Management in the AI-Enhanced Learning Environment

Integrating AI into the classroom isn't just about enhancing educational outcomes; it's also a transformative shift in how classrooms are managed daily. As you begin to fold AI tools into your teaching practices, it's imperative to rethink and revise classroom management strategies to ensure they align with the new digital dynamics. This includes setting new norms and rules, leveraging AI for behavior monitoring, enhancing student engagement, and embedding digital citizenship principles into daily activities.

Adapt Classroom Rules and Norms

The infusion of AI tools into the classroom necessitates updating the existing rules and norms to address the nuances of digital tool usage. It's crucial to establish clear guidelines regarding the use of devices and the handling of data. For instance, you should set specific rules about when and how students can use AI-powered devices, ensuring that their use supports learning objectives rather than distracts from them. Additionally, given the sensitivity of data involved in using AI tools—ranging from personal information to academic records—it's vital to educate students on the importance of data privacy. This includes instructing them on secure login practices, not sharing personal passwords, and understanding what data is being collected through their interactions with AI tools. By updating classroom norms and rules to address these aspects, you can create a secure and efficient environment conducive to integrating AI technologies.

Leverage AI for Behavior Monitoring

AI technology offers sophisticated tools that can assist in monitoring classroom behavior, which can be particularly helpful in oversized or particularly active classes. Systems equipped with attention-tracking capabilities can provide analytics that pinpoint which students are engaged and which ones might be struggling with the material presented. These systems analyze eye movements and facial expressions to gauge engagement levels, providing real-time feedback to educators. This kind of data can be instrumental in adjusting teaching methods and interactions to recapture the attention of disengaged students and ensure the class remains on track. Additionally, AI-driven behavior analytics can help identify patterns that might indicate broader issues, such as learning difficulties or social challenges, enabling timely intervention tailored to individual student needs.

Enhance Engagement through AI

AI's capability to personalize learning experiences is one of its most powerful features in the educational context. By using AI-driven platforms that adapt to each student's academic level and learning style, you can significantly boost engagement and participation. These platforms can modify the difficulty level of tasks based on the student's performance or suggest alternative resources when a student struggles with a concept. For example, an AI learning platform might offer interactive, gamified learning modules to a student who thrives on visual learning and hands-on activities while providing detailed reading material to another student who learns best through textual information. This personalization ensures that each student remains engaged with the curriculum in a manner that suits their learning preferences, thereby enhancing their overall educational experience.

Train in Digital Citizenship

Digital citizenship is an essential skill in today's increasingly digital world, and its importance is amplified in classrooms where AI tools are used. Teaching digital citizenship involves helping students understand their rights and responsibilities in the digital world, which includes respecting others' privacy, understanding the impact of their digital footprints, recognizing and responding to cyberbullying, and using online resources responsibly. Integrating these principles into daily teaching practices is important, making them a natural part of students' learning experiences. This prepares students to use AI tools ethically and responsibly and equips them with the skills they need to navigate the broader digital world safely and effectively.

Incorporating AI into your classroom management strategies doesn't just change how you handle daily tasks; it fundamentally enhances the learning environment. By setting updated norms, using AI to monitor and boost engagement, and embedding digital citizenship into your curriculum, you create a dynamic classroom setting that is both modern and mindful of the challenges and opportunities that technology brings. This approach ensures that AI tools are used to their fullest potential, fostering an educational atmosphere that is engaging, secure, and conducive to learning.

3.4 Using AI to Enhance Group Work and Collaborative Projects

In the evolving educational arena, the ability to work collaboratively on projects is not just a skill but a necessity. Introducing AI into this dynamic changes the playing field by enabling more structured and effective group interactions and project management. AI tools specifically designed to analyze student performance and learning styles can significantly enhance the way educators form groups, ensuring that these groups are balanced and poised for success.

Facilitate Smart Grouping

The traditional method of forming student groups often relies on either random assignment or subjective teacher judgment, which can lead to unbalanced groups where some students may dominate while others may not participate as effectively. AI introduces a more strategic approach called *'smart grouping.'* This technique utilizes algorithms to analyze past performance, learning styles, and even social dynamics to group students in a way that maximizes collective strengths and mitigates weaknesses. For instance, an AI tool might identify students who excel in research and pair them with those who are better at presentation skills, thereby creating a balanced group that can leverage diverse talents. This optimizes the group's overall performance and enhances individual learning experiences by exposing students to new roles and perspectives.

Enhance Collaborative Tools

Beyond group formation, AI can significantly improve the tools used for project collaboration. Platforms that integrate AI can facilitate smoother communication and project management among students. These platforms often feature AI-driven chatbots that can answer questions, suggest resources, and remind students of deadlines. They also include intelligent document management systems that organize project materials automatically and suggest edits or improvements to written content. For instance, an AI-powered collaboration platform could analyze the group's project draft in real time, proposing changes to improve clarity or flagging sections that may need more comprehensive data support. This kind of immediate, actionable feedback is invaluable in a learning environment, as it helps students understand and correct their mistakes promptly, enhancing the learning process.

Track Group Progress with AI

Keeping track of each group's progress in real time can be a logistical challenge, especially for educators managing multiple groups simultaneously. AI comes to the rescue by providing tools that offer real-time analytics on group projects. These tools can track how much each student contributes to the project, monitor milestones, and even predict potential hurdles based on the pace and nature of the group's progress. This not only helps educators intervene more effectively when a group may be lagging but also provides valuable insights into the dynamics and productivity of each group. For example, if a group is consistently missing deadlines, the AI system could automatically flag this issue, allowing the instructor to provide specific resources or support to help the group improve.

Share Best Practices

Drawing from various educational settings, several best practices emerge for integrating AI tools that enhance group work and collaboration. One best practice is continuous training for students and educators on the effective use of AI tools. Regular workshops or training sessions help users understand the features and potential of AI collaborative platforms, ensuring they are used to their full potential.

Another best practice is the establishment of clear guidelines on how AI tools should be used during group projects. These guidelines help maintain a focus on ethical use of technology, respect for data privacy, and ensuring a balanced contribution from all group members.

These AI-enhanced collaborative practices are already showing positive results in various educational settings. For instance, a European university implemented an AI system to track the progress of group projects in a business course. The system provided students and instructors with detailed analytics on group performance, significantly improving the final project outcomes. The students appreciated the immediate feedback and clear benchmarks, which helped them stay on track throughout the semester.

Incorporating AI into group work and collaborative projects presents a unique opportunity to enhance educational outcomes through technology. By facilitating smart grouping, enhancing collaborative tools, tracking group progress, and sharing best practices, AI can make the collaborative process more dynamic, insightful, and productive. This not only prepares students for a workforce that increasingly relies on digital collaboration tools but also enhances their ability to work effectively in teams, a critical skill in both academic and professional settings.

3.5 Overcoming Resistance to AI Tools Among Educators and Students

The prospect of incorporating AI in educational environments is exciting, but it often comes with its share of skepticism and resistance from both educators and students. To handle these challenges effectively, it's imperative to address underlying fears and misconceptions, involve key stakeholders in decision-making processes, and clearly articulate the benefits and successful applications of AI in education.

Address Fears and Misconceptions

The initial step in reducing resistance is addressing the fears and misconceptions surrounding AI technologies. Misunderstandings can range from concerns about AI leading to job losses for teachers to fears about the invasion of privacy or the dehumanization of education. It's important to provide clear, factual information to demystify these technologies. For instance, educators should be reassured that AI is designed to augment their roles, not replace them, by automating administrative tasks and personalizing learning experiences, which can enrich the teaching environment. For students, emphasis should be on how AI tools can offer customized learning experiences and support, such as through tutoring systems that adapt to their unique learning pace and style, making education more effective and enjoyable.

Hosting informational sessions, distributing easy-to-understand literature on AI capabilities and limitations, and openly discussing the ethical use of artificial intelligence in education can help build a foundational understanding and trust in these technologies.

Involve Stakeholders in the Decision-Making Process

Inclusion in the decision-making process is key to fostering acceptance and enthusiasm for AI tools within educational settings. When both educators and students are involved in selecting and implementing AI technologies, they are more likely to feel a sense of ownership and commitment to successfully integrating these tools. This process can take the form of pilot programs where a select group of teachers and students test different AI tools and provide feedback on their experiences. Schools could also form committees or focus groups that include a diverse range of stakeholders to evaluate potential AI solutions. This collaborative approach not only ensures that the chosen tools meet the actual needs of users but also mitigates fears by giving both educators and students a clear voice in how AI is integrated into their educational environment.

Highlight Benefits and Opportunities

Communicating the tangible benefits of AI integration is essential in shifting perceptions and gaining broader acceptance. Focus discussions on how AI can significantly reduce the time teachers spend on grading and administrative tasks, thereby allowing them more time to engage in direct teaching and student support. For students, highlight AI's role in providing personalized learning adjustments that cater to their strengths and weaknesses, which can help improve their academic performance and overall learning experience. It's also beneficial to point out how AI competency is becoming an increasingly important skill in the workforce and familiarity with these tools can provide students with a competitive edge in their future career endeavors.

Provide Success Stories and Testimonials

Nothing speaks louder than success. Sharing stories and testimonials from other schools where AI tools have been successfully integrated can serve as powerful motivators. These narratives should focus on both qualitative and quantitative benefits observed post-AI integration, such as improved student test scores, enhanced engagement levels, reduced workload for teachers, and positive feedback from the school community. Videos, blog posts, or presentations delivered by peers from other institutions can make these success stories more relatable and persuasive.

Seeing and hearing about real-life examples where AI has made a concrete difference can help alleviate concerns and inspire confidence among educators and students alike.

By systematically addressing concerns, involving stakeholders in the decision-making process, highlighting the benefits, and sharing success stories, resistance to AI tools in educational settings can be significantly reduced. This approach facilitates smoother integration of AI technologies and ensures that their potential is fully realized, enhancing educational outcomes and experiences for all involved.

3.6 Safety Protocols and Best Practices for AI in Schools

In an era where AI is becoming a staple in educational environments, the importance of implementing stringent safety protocols and best practices cannot be overstated. As you integrate AI tools into your school, it is essential to establish robust frameworks that ensure the security and privacy of all stakeholders involved. This entails crafting clear data privacy policies, implementing strong security measures, educating about online safety, and regularly updating safety protocols to keep pace with technological advancements.

Establish Clear Data Privacy Policies

The first step in safeguarding your educational environment is establishing clear and comprehensive data privacy policies. These policies should detail how student and staff data will be collected, used, stored, and protected. These policies must comply with local and international data protection regulations, such as the *General Data Protection Regulation (GDPR)* in Europe or the *Family Educational Rights and Privacy Act (FERPA)* in the United States.

It would help if you collaborated with legal experts specializing in data privacy to develop these policies. Additionally, it's crucial to communicate these policies transparently to all members of the school community, ensuring that students, parents, and staff understand their rights and the measures in place to protect their personal information. This transparency builds trust and fosters a culture of accountability and safety around the use of AI tools in education.

Implement Robust Security Measures

With the integration of AI tools that connect to the internet and handle sensitive data, robust security measures are simply non-negotiable. These measures should include, but are not limited to, regular software updates and patches to protect against vulnerabilities, secure data storage practices, and robust encryption protocols to safeguard data transmission. Additionally, schools should invest in cybersecurity solutions such as firewalls and anti-virus software to defend against potential cyber threats. Regular security audits and vulnerability assessments can also help identify and mitigate risks before they can be exploited. It's also wise to have a response plan in place for potential data breaches, ensuring that you can act swiftly to mitigate damages and notify affected parties as required by law.

Educate on Online Safety

Another critical aspect of integrating AI tools in schools is educating both educators and students on online safety practices. This education should cover topics such as secure internet use, recognition of phishing attacks, and safe sharing of personal information. Given that AI tools often require internet connectivity, understanding the landscape of online threats and knowing how to protect oneself is crucial. Schools can integrate this training into the curriculum or offer dedicated workshops and seminars. Additionally, promoting a culture of mindfulness around online interactions and encouraging responsible behavior can significantly enhance the overall cybersecurity posture of your educational institution.

Regularly Review and Update Safety Protocols

Finally, the dynamic nature of technology and the continual evolution of cyber threats necessitate regular reviews and updates of your safety protocols. This ongoing process ensures that your strategies remain practical and relevant. Schools should establish a bi-annual or annual routine to review their AI safety protocols and make necessary adjustments in response to new technological developments and emerging threats. This proactive approach not only helps maintain a high standard of safety but also ensures that the institution remains compliant with evolving legal requirements.

Incorporating these safety protocols and best practices is not just about compliance and protection; it is about creating a secure and nurturing environment where educational AI tools can be used effectively to enhance learning outcomes. By prioritizing safety, schools can harness the benefits of AI with confidence, knowing that they are prepared to tackle the challenges that come with these advanced technologies.

In conclusion, this chapter underscores the critical importance of safety protocols in the AI-enhanced educational world. By establishing clear data privacy policies, implementing robust security measures, educating on online safety, and regularly updating safety protocols, schools can create a secure environment conducive to the effective and safe use of AI tools.

Moving forward, these practices will protect and enhance the educational experience, allowing students and educators to leverage AI technologies with assurance and confidence. Next, we explore how AI transforms educational assessment and evaluation, further revolutionizing how learning outcomes are measured and achieved.

Chapter 4
Personalized Learning and AI

Picture entering a classroom where the buzz of dynamic learning fills the air—a place where every student is engaged not just by the subject matter but by the way it's uniquely delivered to match their individual learning style and pace. This is the promise of personalized learning powered by AI, a promise that is transforming educational paradigms to create learning experiences that are (and should be) as unique as each student who partakes in them.

4.1 Building Adaptive Learning Systems: The Role of AI

Adaptive learning systems are at the forefront of educational innovation, offering a bespoke educational experience that adjusts to each student's needs in real time. These sophisticated AI-driven systems analyze a myriad of data points from student interactions—answers given, time taken, preferences shown—and use this data to tailor the educational content to fit the precise needs of each learner. This dynamic adjustment process ensures that the learning material is always at the right level of difficulty, effectively challenging students to grow without overwhelming them.

How the Mechanism Works

The core of adaptive learning technology lies in its algorithms, which are designed to process inputs from student interactions within the learning platform. These algorithms apply machine learning techniques to discern patterns and learning trajectories, adjusting the course content dynamically. For instance, if a student excels in numerical reasoning but struggles with spatial awareness, the AI system can introduce more visual-spatial activities to bolster understanding while continuing to engage with numerical exercises at a level that keeps the student challenged but not discouraged.

System Integration

Integrating these adaptive systems with existing *Learning Management Systems (LMS)* is of the essence for achieving seamless functionality. This integration allows for a fluid flow of data across platforms, ensuring that all student progress tracked by the AI system is accurately reflected in the broader educational framework used by the school. To facilitate this integration, many AI learning platforms offer *APIs (Application Programming Interfaces)* that enable secure and efficient data exchange between the AI system and the LMS. This connectivity helps maintain comprehensive learning records and provides educators with actionable insights that can inform further instructional design and intervention.

Considering Customization Options

Customization is a cornerstone of adaptive learning systems, empowering educators to align AI functionalities with specific curriculum goals and teaching styles. Educators can set parameters that guide the focus of

AI adjustments, whether on mastering certain skills, improving pace, or deepening conceptual understanding. Additionally, the flexibility of these systems allows for incorporating various instructional materials—videos, interactive simulations, text—to cater to different learning modalities, ensuring that all students find engaging and effective ways to learn according to their preferences.

Benefits of Adaptive Learning Systems

A growing body of research and real-world applications backs the benefits of adaptive learning systems. Schools implementing these technologies report significant improvements in student engagement and performance. For example, a study involving an adaptive mathematics platform showed that students who used the system outperformed their peers on standardized tests, with the greatest gains observed among students who had previously struggled with math. Beyond academic performance, adaptive learning systems also contribute to greater educational equity by ensuring that all students can access personalized support and resources that address their specific learning needs regardless of their starting level.

◊ Interactive Element: Adaptive Learning Systems

Evaluate how adaptive learning systems might change your approach to teaching and reflect on the potential impacts on your students' engagement and understanding. What excites you about such forms of AI? What concerns might you have? Writing down your thoughts on these matters can help you to clarify your perspective on adaptive learning technologies and envision practical ways they could be integrated into your teaching practice.

In this exploration of adaptive learning systems, we've seen how AI is not just reshaping the tools used to educate but also fundamentally transforming the very nature of learning itself. By making education more responsive to the individual needs of each student, AI is enabling a form of teaching that is as inclusive as it is effective. As we continue to uncover the capabilities of AI in education, it becomes clear that these technologies hold not just the promise of a more personalized learning experience but the promise of a brighter educational future for all students as well.

4.2 AI-Driven Assessment Tools for Real-Time Feedback

In the changing realm of academics, the adoption of AI-driven assessment tools is redefining how feedback is delivered in the classroom. These innovative technologies, including automated grading systems and instant quiz analysis platforms, are designed to provide immediate feedback to both students and educators. The real-time nature of this feedback transforms the learning experience, allowing for quick adjustments and fostering a dynamic educational environment where students can thrive.

Automated grading systems utilize advanced algorithms to assess student submissions rapidly. These systems can evaluate various responses, from multiple-choice questions to more complex written answers. By automating the grading process, these tools save valuable time for educators and provide students with prompt feedback on their performance, highlighting areas of strength and pinpointing aspects that require more attention. Instant quiz analysis further complements these systems by offering real-time insights during assessments, enabling students to understand their mistakes immediately and educators to gauge the effectiveness of their instructional methods instantaneously.

This immediate understanding allows both students and teachers to make adjustments on the fly, enhancing the overall learning process and ensuring that no student falls behind due to delayed feedback.

Advantages of Immediate Feedback

The advantages of immediate feedback are profound. By receiving instant responses to their answers, students can quickly identify and correct their misconceptions, which reinforces learning and improves retention. This immediacy helps maintain students' momentum and interest in the subject matter, preventing frustration that can occur from waiting for delayed feedback. For educators, the advantage lies in tracking students' understanding in real time. This ongoing assessment allows teachers to adapt their teaching strategies to address common pitfalls or misconceptions, ensuring their instructional approach is as effective as possible. Moreover, immediate feedback fosters a more responsive and engaging classroom environment, encouraging active participation and making learning more interactive.

Implementation Guidance

Integrating AI-driven assessment tools into regular teaching activities requires careful planning and consideration of technical requirements and educational objectives. Firstly, choosing the right tools that align with your curriculum and assessment strategies is crucial. Once the appropriate tools are selected, the next step involves setting up the technical infrastructure to support these technologies. This setup might include upgrading computer systems, ensuring reliable internet connectivity, and installing necessary software. Training is another critical component of successful implementation. Educators must be thoroughly trained not only in how to use these tools effectively but also in interpreting the data they generate.

This training ensures that teachers can leverage the full potential of AI-driven assessments to enhance their teaching and provide targeted support to their students.

Address Data Privacy Concerns

While the benefits of AI-driven assessment tools are significant, addressing the data privacy concerns associated with their use is essential. These tools often collect and analyze a vast amount of student data, raising issues once again around data security and privacy. To mitigate these concerns, it is imperative to implement stringent data protection measures. This includes using encryption to secure data, ensuring that the AI systems comply with relevant data protection regulations, and maintaining transparency with students and parents about what data is being collected and how it is being used. Additionally, educators should be trained in best practices for data privacy to prevent unauthorized access and ensure that student information is handled responsibly.

Incorporating AI-driven assessment tools into the educational process offers a range of benefits that can significantly enhance teaching and learning. By providing real-time feedback, these tools help create a more dynamic and responsive learning environment where students can continually adjust their learning strategies, and teachers can tailor their instructional methods to meet the needs of their students. However, successfully integrating these technologies requires careful consideration of technical and ethical issues, ensuring they complement existing teaching practices and uphold the highest data privacy standards.

As we continue to explore the numerous purposes of AI in education, these tools represent a powerful means of transforming assessment into a more effective and engaging component of the educational experience.

4.3 Case Studies: Successful Personalized Learning Models Using AI

Across the globe, the integration of AI into personalized learning strategies has transformed educational landscapes, offering tailored learning experiences that cater to the unique needs of every student. From rural schools in Africa to advanced learning centers in Silicon Valley, AI's role in education has shown remarkable versatility and effectiveness. In this paragraph, I will share with you a few case studies that highlight how AI has been successfully implemented in diverse educational settings, providing valuable insights into the key factors that contribute to its success.

In Sweden, a notable project involved using an AI-driven platform in a public school to enhance language learning among immigrants. The AI system was designed to adapt to each student's proficiency level, offering personalized exercises and interactive sessions that improved both language skills and cultural integration. The success of this model was largely due to the robust technological infrastructure that supported seamless AI functionality and real-time data analytics. This infrastructure allowed educators to continuously monitor progress and adjust learning modules to meet students' individual needs better. Moreover, extensive training was provided to teachers to ensure they were adept at utilizing the AI tools, which enhanced their ability to support their students effectively.

Another compelling example comes from Japan, where an AI-powered system was implemented in a high school to support students with mathematics. The system used sophisticated algorithms to analyze students' learning habits and performance, adjusting the difficulty of problems and the pace of instruction accordingly. This personalized approach helped students grasp complex mathematical concepts at their own pace, markedly improving their overall performance. The key to this success was integrating the AI system with the school's existing LMS, which ensured that all student data was centrally managed and easily accessible to both students and teachers. The adaptability of the AI system was also crucial, as it was able to accommodate different teaching styles and curriculum requirements, making it a versatile tool for educators.

In South Africa, a rural school with limited resources implemented a low-cost AI solution to enhance reading skills among young learners. Despite the challenging infrastructure, the AI tool provided interactive reading exercises accessible via mobile devices, offering students engaging and effective literacy training. The scalability of this AI model was particularly noteworthy, as it allowed for easy expansion to other schools within the region without the need for extensive technological upgrades. The success of this initiative underscored the adaptability of AI solutions to various educational contexts and constraints, demonstrating that even schools with limited resources could benefit from AI technologies.

From these case studies, several lessons can be drawn that are applicable to educators and policymakers worldwide:

1. A solid technological foundation is essential, as it ensures the smooth operation and scalability of AI systems.

2. Training educators on using AI tools is crucial for maximizing their potential and ensuring that they complement traditional teaching methods.

3. The adaptability of AI systems to different educational environments and teaching styles is essential for their successful integration and effectiveness.

4. The commitment to continuous evaluation and adjustment of AI strategies based on real-time feedback and data analytics leads to sustained improvement in learning outcomes.

These global examples not only illustrate the transformative potential of AI in personalizing education but also highlight the practical considerations and strategic approaches that contribute to the successful implementation of AI in diverse learning environments. These case studies provide valuable insights and inspiration for leveraging technology to meet the varied needs of students around the world, making education more inclusive, effective, and personalized.

4.4 Addressing Diverse Learning Needs Through AI

In education, diversity is not just a buzzword but a critical component that reflects the varied dimensions of human potential across different backgrounds, abilities, and interests. With its capability to analyze vast amounts of data and adapt to individual needs, AI presents a unique opportunity to cater to this diversity more effectively than ever before. Educators can create a more inclusive and supportive learning environment by employing specific AI tools designed to address a broad spectrum of learning needs.

AI tools such as *Text-to-Speech (TTS)* and *Speech Recognition* technologies are revolutionizing the way students with different needs engage with educational content. TTS tools, for example, can help students with visual impairments or reading difficulties by converting written text into spoken words, thus providing them access to written materials in an audible format. On the other hand, Speech Recognition technology assists students with physical disabilities affecting their ability to write or use a keyboard by enabling them to dictate responses and interact with digital learning platforms using voice commands. Another innovative tool is the use of AI-driven educational games that adapt to students' cognitive levels and learning speeds, which can be particularly beneficial for gifted learners who require more challenging content to stay engaged.

How Customization Works

The true power of AI in education lies in its ability to be customized. Educators can utilize AI to develop learning plans that are not only aligned with the curriculum but also tailored to the strengths and weaknesses of each student. This customization is made possible through AI's data-processing capabilities, which allow it to analyze individual learning patterns and preferences. For instance, if an AI system notices that a student excels in visual learning but struggles with textual information, it can automatically adjust to provide more visual aids and fewer text-heavy materials for that student. Similarly, for students with language barriers, AI can modify the language level of the instruction or provide additional language support where necessary. This level of customization ensures that each student can learn in a way that best suits their individual needs, thereby enhancing their overall educational experience.

How AI Promotes Inclusivity in Education

Inclusivity in education ensures that every student has an equal opportunity to learn and succeed, regardless of their circumstances. AI is vital in promoting inclusivity by leveling the educational playing field. It does this by providing tools that adapt to the needs of each student, giving everyone the support they require to achieve their potential. For example, AI-powered platforms can offer real-time language translation services that help non-native speakers understand the curriculum in their preferred language. Additionally, AI can identify patterns that may indicate a student is at risk of falling behind and can initiate additional support to address these issues before they become significant barriers to learning.

Practical Examples of Successful Customization by AI

Consider the case of an inner-city school that implemented an AI-driven platform to support students with varying levels of English proficiency. The platform identified students struggling with language barriers and provided customized lessons that included both language learning and subject matter instruction. This dual approach helped improve the students' English language skills while ensuring they stayed caught up in other subjects. As a result, the school saw improved test scores and decreased dropout rates among non-native speakers.

Another example is a rural school district that utilized AI to support students with dyslexia. The district employed a tool that used AI to analyze each student's reading patterns and identify specific challenges. Based on this analysis, the tool provided personalized reading exercises that focused on individual difficulties, adapting the level of challenge as the students improved. This targeted support helped students with dyslexia not only improve their reading skills but also gain confidence in their ability to learn alongside their peers, thus positively contributing to their overall self-esteem.

These examples illustrate how AI is being used to bridge gaps in education, providing targeted support where it is most needed and ensuring that all students, regardless of their challenges, have the opportunity to succeed. The role AI plays in fostering an inclusive and equitable educational environment is only expected to grow, transforming the landscape of academics in ways that were once unimaginable.

4.5 The Impact of AI on Special Education

In the realm of special education, AI is not just a tool for enhancement but a transformative force that redefines the educational realm for students with special needs. Consider the dynamic capabilities of speech recognition technologies, which have profoundly impacted students with speech impairments. These AI-driven applications allow for voice-to-text functionality, enabling students who face challenges in articulating words to engage in classroom activities, communicate with peers, and express their thoughts and knowledge through written text generated from their spoken words. This technology integrates students more fully into the educational process and bolsters their confidence and independence.

Similarly transformative are AI tutors especially designed for students with learning difficulties. These intelligent systems are tailored to adapt to the individual learning pace and style of each student, providing personalized instruction that can pinpoint specific areas of difficulty and continuously adjust the teaching approach accordingly. For a student struggling with dyscalculia, for instance, an AI tutor can modify numerical teaching methods, employ visual aids, or interactively work through problems to make abstract concepts more concrete and understandable. The real-time adaptation and patient, personalized interaction that AI tutors offer can make a significant difference in overcoming learning obstacles.

Advantages of AI in Special Education

The benefits of incorporating AI in special education are substantial and multifaceted. By providing tools that compensate for or mitigate learning impairments, AI technologies facilitate more effective and inclusive educational experiences. Students with disabilities receive precisely the kind of support they need when they need it, allowing for a more equitable educational opportunity. Educators, too, find great value in AI's capacity to offer detailed insights into each student's progress and challenges, which informs more effective teaching strategies and interventions. Moreover, the continuous adaptation and personalized learning paths created by AI can significantly improve academic achievement and personal growth for special education students, as these tools cater directly to their unique learning needs.

Teacher and Caregiver Roles

The introduction of AI in special education also necessitates a reevaluation of the roles of educators and caregivers. Far from replacing the human element, AI supports and enhances the irreplaceable human interactions critical in special education. Teachers are freed from some of the more time-consuming tasks, such as grading and progress tracking, allowing them to dedicate more time to one-on-one instruction and to develop deeper, more empathetic relationships with their students. Caregivers and parents find that AI tools provide better insights into their children's educational progress and challenges, enabling them to be more effective advocates and supporters of their children's education. However, this shift also requires that educators and caregivers adapt to new technologies, incorporating AI tools into their teaching methods and interaction with students, which can involve a significant learning curve.

Special Education: Ethical and Practical Considerations

The integration of AI into special education, while beneficial, is not without its ethical and practical challenges. One of the primary considerations is ensuring the accessibility of these technologies. AI tools must be designed to be easily used by all students, including those with severe disabilities who may require specialized interfaces or adaptive hardware. Additionally, the customization of AI technologies can raise concerns about data privacy, as significant amounts of personal and sensitive information are often needed to tailor learning experiences effectively. Educators and technology providers must ensure that data is handled securely and that privacy regulations are strictly followed.

Moreover, there is a challenge in ensuring that AI tools do not become a one-size-fits-all solution but are used as part of a broader educational strategy that includes traditional teaching methods and human oversight. Training for teachers is crucial, not only in the use of AI technology but in integrating these tools into their existing teaching practices in a way that respects and enhances the established educational goals and standards.

In essence, AI has the potential to significantly enhance educational outcomes for students with special needs by providing personalized, adaptable learning tools. However, successfully implementing these technologies in special teaching requires careful consideration of ethical issues, practical challenges, and the ongoing role of educators and caregivers. As it undergoes further development and becomes more integrated into educational settings, AI promises to open new pathways for accessibility and learning in special education, creating more inclusive environments that recognize and cater to the diverse needs of all students.

4.6 Predictive Analytics in Education: Forecasting Learning Outcomes

Predictive analytics in education is a revolutionary approach that leverages historical data and sophisticated AI algorithms to anticipate future learning outcomes and trends. This methodology transforms vast amounts of past student performance data into insightful, actionable forecasts that can significantly enhance educational strategies and interventions. At its core, predictive analytics involves extracting patterns from past data to predict future outcomes. For instance, by analyzing past exam scores, participation rates, and homework completion rates, predictive analytics can identify potential academic risks and successes before they manifest, thus allowing for timely interventions that can dramatically alter a student's educational trajectory. Basically, this incredible technology enables educators to be several steps ahead of their own teaching practices at all times.

Real-World Applications of Predictive Analytics

There are many real-world applications of predictive analytics in schools that are compelling and illustrative of the technology's potential to transform educational environments. For example, some schools utilize predictive analytics to identify students who are at risk of dropping out. By analyzing patterns in attendance, behavior, and grades, these systems can flag students who exhibit signs of disengagement or academic trouble early on. This allows educators to intervene with tailored support programs, such as tutoring or counseling, potentially steering these students back on track toward successful educational outcomes. Another application can be found in curriculum development, where predictive analytics helps in understanding which parts of a course are failing to engage students or are too challenging. This insight enables educators to adjust the curriculum dynamically, enhancing its effectiveness and relevance.

In another case, schools use predictive analytics to optimize learning paths for individual students. By understanding a student's learning habits and historical academic performance, AI systems can recommend personalized learning activities and resources that maximize learning efficiency and outcomes. This targeted approach boosts individual performance and helps allocate educational resources more effectively, ensuring that each student receives the attention and support they need to excel.

Data Requirements

Effective predictive analytics hinges on the quality and granularity of the data collected. Essential data types include demographic information, academic records, attendance logs, behavior incident reports, and engagement metrics from learning platforms. Collecting this data involves a systematic approach where accuracy and consistency are paramount. Data processing and analysis practices also play a critical role. This includes cleaning the data to remove inaccuracies, normalizing diverse data formats, and employing robust statistical methods to ensure reliable predictions. Schools must also invest in secure and scalable data storage solutions to handle the large volumes of data required for effective predictive analytics.

Ethical Implications of Predictive Analysis

While predictive analytics can offer substantial benefits in education, it also raises significant ethical concerns that must be addressed. Privacy issues are at the forefront, as predictive analytics (just like other AI technologies employed in education) relies on detailed personal information about students. Schools must ensure that data collection and usage comply with privacy laws and ethical standards and that students and parents are informed about how their data is used. Needless to say, transparency is of the essence here. There is also the risk of bias in predictive models, where algorithms might inadvertently perpetuate historical inequalities or biases in the data. To mitigate these risks, it's crucial to regularly audit and update AI models to ensure fairness and accuracy and to implement transparency measures that allow for the independent review of algorithmic decisions.

In this exploration of predictive analytics, we uncover its potential to anticipate educational outcomes and actively shape them for the better. By utilizing historical data and AI algorithms, educators can provide interventions that are precisely timed and tailored, significantly enhancing student success and educational efficiency. Without a doubt, predictive analytics make for a powerful tool that promises to alter the realm of education by making it more responsive and attuned to the needs of every student.

As we wrap up this chapter on predictive analytics, we're reminded of the transformative power of data in shaping educational futures. This journey through the mechanisms, applications, and implications of predictive analytics underscores its role as a critical tool in modern education—helping to forecast and thereby forge better pathways for student success. To educators, embracing this technology means not only predicting the future but actively participating in molding it to ensure optimal learning outcomes for all students. Moving forward, the insights gleaned from predictive analytics will continue to influence educational strategies, making learning a process of discovery and creation.

You may have noticed that ethical considerations are a recurring theme throughout this book. I deliberately made it so because without them, AI could never be integrated responsibly into education, much less gain the trust of all stakeholders involved. I actually find this topic so important that I decided to dedicate an entire chapter to it, which is up next.

Make a Difference in Education with Your Review

Unlock the Power of Generosity in Academics

"Teaching is the greatest act of optimism. Generosity in education means sharing knowledge and fostering growth in every student, believing in their potential to create a better world." - Colleen Wilcox

I strive to make AI in education understandable and accessible to every teacher, student, and administrator. Everything I have done to write this book stems from that mission. And, the only way for me to accomplish that mission is by reaching... Well, everyone.

This is where you come in. Most people do, in fact, judge a book by its cover (and its reviews). So here's my ask on behalf of a curious educator, student, or administrator you've never met:

Please help them by leaving this book a review.

Your gift costs no money and less than 60 seconds to make real, but it can change someone else's life forever.

Your review could help...

- ...one more teacher inspire their students.

- ...one more school embrace AI ethically.

- ...one more administrator streamline tasks.

- ...one more classroom transformation with AI.

- ...one more educational dream come true.

To help this person for real, all you have to do is take less than 60 seconds to leave a review. You can do so by simply scanning the QR code below:

Thank you from the bottom of my heart. Now, back to our regularly scheduled programming.

Your biggest fan,

Edward Foster

Chapter 5

Ethical and Policy Considerations

———◆◇◆———

As the dawn of AI in education ushers in unprecedented opportunities for enhancing learning experiences, it simultaneously casts a spotlight on the ethical scaffolding required to uphold the integrity and privacy of the very individuals it seeks to benefit. Navigating this new terrain involves a delicate balance, ensuring that while we embrace the vast capabilities of AI, we remain vigilant guardians of the principle that all this marvelous technology is to be used exclusively for benevolent purposes. This chapter delves into the crucial aspects of data privacy, a cornerstone in the ethical application of AI in educational settings, highlighting the responsibilities and strategies necessary to protect sensitive information and maintain a transparent relationship with all parties involved.

5.1 Data Privacy and AI: Protecting Student Information

In the digital age, data is often likened to currency, and in the context of education, this data assumes a profoundly sensitive nature. Student information, from academic records to personal details, is not merely data points; they are reflections of individual identities and potentials. The sensitivity of this information mandates stringent protocols to ensure its protection. As you integrate AI systems into your educational practices, recognizing the profound responsibility to safeguard student data is paramount. This involves securing the data from external threats and managing it with the highest standards of integrity and care. Each piece of data should be handled as if it were a trustee of a student's future. These warranting measures go beyond compliance to embody a commitment to safeguarding student privacy.

Implementation of Robust Security Measures

Securing student data in an AI-enhanced educational environment involves a multifaceted approach. Encryption is the first line of defense, ensuring that data, whether at rest or in transit, is shielded from unauthorized access. However, securing data extends beyond encryption. Implementing access controls is crucial; not everyone needs to access all data types. By ensuring that only authorized personnel have access to specific types of sensitive information, the risk of accidental breaches or misuse is significantly reduced. Regular audits and security assessments also play a critical role in this strategy. They help identify vulnerabilities in the system and gauge the effectiveness of current security measures, providing insights into where improvements can be made. These practices are not static but must evolve continually as new threats emerge and technologies advance.

Legal Compliance

Traversing the legal landscape of data privacy involves adhering to a complex array of regulations that vary by region, such as the *General Data Protection Regulation (GDPR)* in Europe and the *Family Educational Rights and Privacy Act (FERPA)* in the United States. These laws provide frameworks that govern the use of student data, but they also offer an opportunity to build trust with stakeholders. Compliance should be seen as a legal obligation and a genuine commitment to ethical responsibility. Educating yourself and your staff about these regulations is crucial. It not only ensures that your educational institution remains on the right side of the law but also reinforces a culture of transparency and accountability in handling student data.

Promote Transparency

Transparency with students and parents about how their data is being collected, used, and protected is crucial. This transparency fosters trust and reassures stakeholders that student data is handled with the utmost respect and care. One effective way to promote transparency is through clear, accessible privacy policies and regular communication with parents and students about any changes in data use practices. Additionally, giving students and parents some control over their data can empower them and reinforce a trust-based relationship. This might include options to view the data collected, request corrections, or even opt out of certain data uses, where feasible.

◊ Interactive Element: Privacy Practices Checklist

To aid you in the rigorous application of data privacy practices, consider the checklist below as a foundational tool:

- **Encryption**: Ensure all sensitive data is encrypted during storage and transmission.

- **Access Controls**: Implement strict access controls and regularly review who has access to what data.

- **Compliance Training**: Regularly train staff on compliance with key data protection regulations like GDPR and FERPA.

- **Audits**: Conduct regular security audits and risk assessments to identify and mitigate potential vulnerabilities.

- **Transparency**: Communicate clearly with stakeholders about how data is used, stored, and protected, and provide mechanisms for feedback and control over personal data.

Through the conscientious application of these strategies, you can navigate the complexities of data privacy in AI-enhanced education with integrity and foresight. By prioritizing the protection of student information, you not only comply with legal standards but also elevate the ethical standards of your educational practices, ensuring that AI is a tool for empowerment rather than a source of frustration and contention.

5.2 Ethical AI Use: Best Practices for Educators

As an educator, your commitment extends beyond delivering knowledge; it encompasses fostering an ethical learning environment where technology serves as an enabler rather than a disruptor. Integrating AI into educational practices brings forth a spectrum of moral considerations that require you to recalibrate your approaches and guidelines. Developing robust ethical guidelines for AI use in the classroom aligns with your educational goals and upholds the broader ethical standards that govern your profession. These guidelines should serve as a compass that guides educators in navigating the complex interplay between technology and education, ensuring that AI tools are used to enhance learning experiences while respecting the dignity and rights of all students.

Creating these guidelines involves a detailed process where you, as an educator, need to consider the implications of AI applications. This includes understanding the capabilities of AI technologies, the contexts in which they can be used effectively, and the potential risks they might pose. For instance, when using AI for personalized learning, guidelines may stipulate how to balance the benefits of customized content with the need to ensure that content does not isolate learners or limit their exposure to diverse perspectives. Additionally, guidelines should address the management of AI systems, including regular updates and checks to ensure that the technology remains a safe and effective tool for education.

Promoting fairness and equity in education by using AI tools is fundamental. This involves ensuring that these tools do not perpetuate or exacerbate existing inequalities within the educational system. To achieve this, it is vital to evaluate AI applications critically before they are integrated into your classroom. Consider whether the AI tool has been trained on diverse data sets that reflect the varied demographics of your student population. This can help mitigate the risk of biased outcomes that could disadvantage certain groups of students. Moreover, it is essential to continuously monitor AI tools' outcomes to ensure they deliver equitable benefits to all students. Should any discrepancies arise, having a protocol to address these inequities swiftly ensures that all students receive a fair educational experience.

Accountability in the use of AI systems in education cannot be overstated. Maintaining human oversight is crucial to ensure that AI tools are used responsibly. While AI can automate many tasks, decisions that significantly impact student welfare should always involve a human element. Educators must understand the workings of AI tools sufficiently to make informed decisions based on the insights these tools provide. This includes interpreting AI-generated data with a critical eye, understanding its limitations, and considering the broader context that might influence the data. For example, if an AI system identifies a student as underperforming, it is essential to look beyond the data points and understand the holistic circumstances affecting the student's performance, which may include factors outside the classroom.

Encouraging ethical training for educators is key to fostering a responsible AI-enhanced educational environment. Training programs should focus on how to use AI tools effectively and understanding the ethical dimensions of AI technology. This includes understanding how AI decisions are made, the biases that can influence AI algorithms, and the ethical implications of deploying AI in diverse educational settings. Such training empowers educators to use AI responsibly and advocate for ethical practices within their institutions. Additionally, these training sessions offer a platform for educators to discuss and share experiences on the ethical use of AI, promoting a collaborative approach to ethical decision-making.

Educators play a lead role in crafting a learning environment enriched by AI, where ethical considerations are as integral as educational outcomes. They can lead by example by developing comprehensive ethical guidelines, advocating for fairness and equity, ensuring accountability, and participating in ongoing ethical training. This approach not only enhances the educational experiences offered to students but also ensures that these experiences are delivered within a framework that respects and uplifts the ethical standards of the educational profession.

AI continues to progress, and so should strategies and commitments to using this technology ethically, ensuring it remains a valuable ally in the quest to educate and inspire the next generation.

5.3 Developing Inclusive AI Policies for Education

Creating inclusive policies in the realm of AI in education encapsulates a vision where every student, irrespective of their background or abilities, benefits equitably from the technological advancements AI brings to the classroom. In crafting such policies, the emphasis must be on inclusivity that reaches beyond mere access, embedding principles that ensure these powerful tools uplift every student, including those who are often marginalized or face disabilities. This vision calls for policies meticulously designed to adapt AI tools to meet a broad spectrum of needs, ensuring that every student is included in the digital leap forward.

Formulating these inclusive policies must begin with a clear understanding of the diverse needs of the student population. This understanding can be deepened through engagements with various stakeholders — students, parents, educators, and community members — who bring different perspectives and insights. Involving these groups in policy discussions enriches the policy-making process with multiple viewpoints and fosters a sense of community ownership of the resultant policies. For instance, parents of students with disabilities can provide firsthand insights into their children's specific challenges, which can be used as a foundation for more targeted and effective policy measures. Similarly, teachers can share observations from the frontline of education, offering valuable feedback on how AI tools perform in real classroom settings.

In order to ensure these policies remain effective as technology and societal needs change, it is crucial to establish mechanisms for their regular review and adaptation. This could involve setting up dedicated committees or task forces that periodically assess the impact of AI policies and recommend adjustments based on the latest technological advancements and educational research. These bodies should be empowered to pilot innovative approaches to AI integration that can address emerging challenges and opportunities, ensuring the policies stay at the cutting edge and continue serving all students' best interests.

To illustrate the effectiveness of inclusive AI policies, consider the example of a school district that implemented an AI-powered learning platform designed to adapt to various learning disabilities. The policy underpinning this implementation was crafted with inputs from special education experts, regular teachers, parents, and even students themselves. The platform was regularly reviewed and updated, with feedback from these stakeholders directly influencing iterations of the AI software. This collaborative and dynamic approach ensured that the platform continuously stayed up-to-date so it could optimally meet the diverse needs of students, ultimately leading to marked improvements in learning outcomes across the board.

In fostering such inclusive environments, the focus must always be on ensuring that AI tools are leveraged to amplify opportunities for all students, particularly those who might otherwise be at a disadvantage. By committing to policies that address current needs and are adaptable to future demands, educators and policymakers can ensure that AI serves as a bridge, rather than a barrier, to educational equity. Through ongoing stakeholder engagement and proactive policy management, AI can be effectively harnessed to create educational experiences that are genuinely inclusive, reflecting the diverse tapestry of learners in our schools.

5.4 The Role of AI in Surveillance and Security in Schools

Integrating AI into school surveillance and security systems presents a modern solution to age-old concerns about safety. However, it also introduces a complex web of ethical considerations and potential risks that must be navigated with care. In schools, AI is increasingly deployed in various forms, from cameras that monitor hallways and common areas to software that oversees students' online activities. These technologies aim to enhance the safety of students by preventing incidents such as bullying, vandalism, and other security breaches. Additionally, AI-driven systems can analyze vast amounts of data from school entry points to better secure the premises against unauthorized visitors.

Despite the obvious benefits, using AI in school surveillance raises significant privacy concerns. The very tools designed to protect students can, paradoxically, infringe upon their privacy. For instance, constant monitoring of students' physical and digital activities might create an atmosphere of surveillance that could impact the school environment, making it feel more like a place of scrutiny than a space for free exploration and learning. The challenge, therefore, lies in employing these technologies in a way that bolsters security without creating a panoptic surveillance system that could stifle the educational experience and infringe on students' privacy rights.

This delicate balance requires a rigorous assessment of the potential benefits and risks associated with deploying AI surveillance in schools. It needs a framework that enhances security and protects students' fundamental rights. Such a framework should be built on the principles of proportionality and necessity, ensuring that surveillance measures are appropriate to the specific risks faced by the school community and that they are the least intrusive means available to achieve security objectives.

Legal considerations also play a major role in shaping the use of AI for surveillance in educational settings. Schools must make their way through a complex landscape of laws and regulations that govern data protection and privacy. In the United States, for example, any implementation of surveillance technologies in schools must comply with federal laws like FERPA, which protects the privacy of student education records. Similarly, in Europe, the GDPR imposes strict requirements on data processing, ensuring that personal data is handled lawfully and transparently. These legal frameworks compel schools to carefully consider how they deploy surveillance technologies and manage the data they collect to avoid legal repercussions and maintain trust within the school community.

Engaging the school community in discussions about AI surveillance is imperative for fostering a collaborative approach to school safety. This involves transparent communication with students, parents, teachers, and other stakeholders about what technologies are being implemented, how they will be used, and the measures in place to protect privacy. Such dialogue can help demystify AI systems for those affected by their use and provide an opportunity to address concerns and gather feedback. Moreover, involving the community in the decision-making process can lead to more informed and acceptable practices that reflect the values and needs of all parties involved.

The use of AI in school surveillance and security is a prime example of how technological advancements can offer significant benefits while also posing new challenges. As schools consider integrating these sophisticated tools into their safety protocols, they must do so with a keen awareness of the ethical implications and a strong commitment to upholding the rights and dignity of all students.

By carefully balancing the benefits of enhanced security with the need to protect privacy and fostering an inclusive dialogue with the school community, educators can ensure that AI is a valuable ally in creating safe and supportive learning environments.

5.5 Addressing Bias in AI Educational Tools

When you implement AI technologies in the classroom, the specter of bias makes for a substantial concern that must be rigorously managed. Despite their advanced algorithms, AI systems are not inherently neutral; they reflect the data on which they are trained. Common sources of bias in AI systems include biased training data and flawed algorithms. For example, if an AI-powered educational tool is predominantly trained on data from a particular demographic, it may not perform as well for students outside that demographic. This can manifest in less accurate assessments or recommendations, potentially disadvantaging students not represented in the training data. Additionally, suppose the algorithms are designed without considering diverse educational needs. In that case, they may inadvertently favor certain learning styles or abilities over others, further embedding bias into the educational process.

A multifaceted strategy is essential to mitigate these biases. Identifying and addressing biases in educational AI tools begins with diversifying the data sets used for training these systems. By ensuring that the data reflects a broad spectrum of populations, including varied ethnicities, genders, socioeconomic backgrounds, and learning abilities, you can help minimize the risk of biased outcomes. It is also crucial to involve data science and educational psychology experts during AI tools' development and training phases to ensure that the algorithms are robust and considerate of educational equity.

Algorithm auditing is another critical strategy. Regular audits of AI algorithms can help identify biases or flaws that might lead to unfair or unequal educational outcomes. These audits should be conducted by independent third parties to ensure objectivity, and the findings should be made transparent to all stakeholders, including students, educators, and parents. This transparency builds trust and fosters a collaborative environment where user feedback can lead to continual improvement of the AI tools.

Promoting diversity in AI development teams is also vital. When the teams designing and developing AI tools are diverse, the products they create are more likely to consider and address a wide range of needs and perspectives. This diversity can be in terms of race, gender, educational background, and professional experience. For example, a team that includes members who have a deep understanding of special education is more likely to develop AI tools that effectively address the needs of students with disabilities.

Monitoring AI tools for signs of bias is essential for ensuring fairness and equity in AI-driven educational tools. This involves initial testing before deployment and ongoing monitoring to see how the AI applications perform in diverse, real-world academic settings. Monitoring should be complemented by feedback mechanisms that allow educators and students to report any issues they perceive in the AI tools' fairness or effectiveness. Based on this feedback, the algorithms can be adjusted to improve their accuracy and fairness across all student groups.

By implementing these strategies, you can help ensure that AI tools serve as a force for equity in education rather than perpetuating existing disparities. This proactive approach to managing bias in AI enhances the educational outcomes for all students and aligns with broader ethical standards that promote fairness and inclusivity in educational practices. With AI's increasingly prominent role in education, the commitment to rigorously addressing bias will remain a cornerstone of ensuring that these powerful technologies benefit every student equally, paving the way for a more inclusive and equitable educational landscape.

5.6 International Guidelines and Standards for AI in Education

Navigating the waters of AI in education demands a global compass, one that is guided by international guidelines and standards designed to ensure that the use of AI technologies fosters an equitable, effective, and ethically sound educational environment. Organizations like *UNESCO* and the *Organisation for Economic Co-operation and Development (OECD)* have been at the forefront of establishing such frameworks. These guidelines serve as a beacon for educators and policymakers worldwide, providing a set of principles that promote the responsible and beneficial use of AI in educational settings.

For instance, the UNESCO recommendations on AI in education emphasize the importance of ensuring inclusive and equitable use of AI technologies. They advocate for AI systems that enhance teacher and student capacities, support lifelong learning, and respect cultural diversity. Similarly, the OECD's *AI Principles* highlight the imperatives of transparency, robustness, and accountability in AI systems, urging that they be designed in a way that respects human rights and democratic values. These international standards are not just abstract ideals; they are practical signposts that guide the implementation of AI technologies in a manner that upholds the dignity and rights of all learners.

For educators and policymakers looking to align their AI strategies with these global standards, the task begins with a thorough understanding of the guidelines. This understanding forms the basis for developing AI policies and practices that comply with international norms and are tailored to the specific educational needs and contexts of their regions. It involves a detailed assessment of how existing or planned AI applications measure up against these standards, identifying areas where adjustments may be necessary to ensure alignment. For instance, if an AI tool used in classrooms is found to lack adequate measures for data protection, steps must be taken to enhance its privacy safeguards to meet the criteria set out by these international frameworks.

Global cooperation is key to effectively establishing and maintaining standards for AI in education. By sharing best practices, resources, and experiences, countries can learn from each other and collectively advance the state of AI in education. This cooperation can take many forms, from international conferences and workshops that facilitate the exchange of ideas to collaborative research projects that develop new AI solutions. Such collaborative efforts enrich the global knowledge base and foster a sense of international solidarity in pursuing educational advancements through AI. For example, a joint research initiative between educational institutions in Asia and Europe could explore the development of AI tools that cater to diverse linguistic and cultural contexts, benefiting students across both continents.

Discussing possible future developments in international guidelines for AI technology is both exciting and essential. As AI systems become more sophisticated and their applications in education more widespread, existing guidelines will likely need to be updated or expanded to address new challenges and opportunities. Issues such as the ethical implications of advanced predictive analytics in student assessments or the integration of AI in early childhood education may require new standards to ensure that these technologies are used responsibly. Anticipating and preparing for these changes is crucial for educators and policymakers, who must stay ahead of the curve to continue providing high-quality, equitable, and ethical education.

In conclusion, the world of AI in education is dynamic, shaped by ongoing technological developments and the continuous evolution of international guidelines and standards. For educators, administrators, and policymakers, staying informed about these guidelines and actively participating in the global dialogue on AI in education is of the essence. It ensures compliance with international standards and the practical and ethical integration of AI technologies that enhance learning experiences and outcomes for students worldwide. The collaborative efforts in shaping these standards will undoubtedly play a critical role in harnessing the full potential of AI to transform education on a global scale.

Chapter 6

Preparing for an AI-Driven Future in Education

———◆○◆———

S o far, I have shared with you several examples of AI technology that are available today. But now, let's pretend we leap forward in time to look at where all these technological advancements are (realistically!) headed. Imagine stepping into a classroom not bounded by walls but by the limitless possibilities of technology. Here, AI does not just support education; it actively shapes its future. To educators and administrators alike, understanding and preparing for this AI-driven future is not just advantageous—it is imperative. In this chapter, we will explore the vibrant frontier of AI in education, highlighting emerging trends, making informed predictions, and discussing the profound implications these advancements hold for educational policy and practice.

6.1 The Future of AI in Education: Trends and Realistic Predictions

Emerging Trends

AI technologies used in education are evolving at an exhilarating pace, marked by significant advancements in *Machine Learning*, *Natural Language Processing (NLP)*, and the rise of educational bots. These technologies are not merely enhancing existing educational practices but are creating new paradigms for how education is delivered and experienced.

Machine Learning algorithms are becoming increasingly sophisticated at processing and understanding vast amounts of educational data, providing previously unattainable insights. This capability allows for the personalization of learning at an unprecedented scale, catering to the needs of individual students in real time.

Natural Language Processing is another area witnessing rapid growth. NLP enables machines to understand and interact with humans in their natural language, not through pre-programmed responses but by understanding human communication's nuances. This technology is essential in developing intelligent tutoring systems that can converse with students, understand their queries, and provide personalized help. Furthermore, the advent of educational bots, or chatbots, is transforming student interactions. These AI-driven programs can guide students through complex learning materials, offer support and tutoring, and even assist, to some degree, with mental health by providing therapeutic conversations.

Realistic Predictions

Looking ahead, these trends suggest several transformative shifts in educational methodologies, environments, and administration. Personalization will likely reach new heights, with AI systems designing learning paths tailored to students' academic needs and emotional and psychological states. Imagine an AI that can predict when a student feels frustrated or confused and modify the lesson to alleviate these feelings, thereby enhancing learning efficiency.

The role of teachers will also evolve in response to these technologies. Rather than being the sole source of knowledge, educators will become facilitators and guides in a more collaborative and interactive learning process powered by AI. Moreover, administrative tasks that currently consume a significant portion of educators' time, such as grading and scheduling, will be more efficiently managed by AI, freeing up teachers to focus more on teaching and less on bureaucratic tasks.

AI Innovations on the Horizon

Groundbreaking projects are already underway that could revolutionize educational practices. For instance, AI systems that use facial recognition to read students' emotions and engagement levels during lessons are being tested. Such technologies can provide immediate feedback to educators about the effectiveness of their teaching strategies and student engagement, enabling real-time adjustments to improve learning outcomes.

Another exciting innovation involves using AI to create dynamic textbooks that adjust content based on a student's mastery of the topic.

These "smart" textbooks can elaborate on concepts that a student is struggling with or skip over material that the student already understands, making learning more efficient and personalized.

Future Implications for Policy and Practice

Integrating these advanced AI technologies in education will require proactive adaptations in policy and practice. Educational institutions must develop new standards and guidelines that address the ethical use of AI, ensure the privacy and security of student data, and promote equitable access to these technologies. For example, policies must be crafted to govern the use of AI's emotional recognition capabilities to ensure it is used ethically and does not infringe on students' privacy.

Furthermore, as AI becomes a fundamental part of the educational world, there will be a growing need for educators to be skilled in teaching, understanding, and managing AI technologies. This shift will necessitate significant changes in teacher education and professional development, emphasizing the importance of technological proficiency alongside pedagogical skills.

In this rapidly evolving world, staying informed about the latest AI advancements and understanding their potential educational applications is crucial for educators and administrators. By embracing these technologies and preparing for their integration into educational practices, you can ensure that you are keeping pace with the changes and actively contributing to shaping the future of education in the AI era.

6.2 Skills That Students Need for an AI-Driven World

In an era increasingly dominated by sophisticated technologies, equipping students with the right skills is essential—not only for their personal success but also for the advancement of society. As AI becomes increasingly embedded in our daily lives, the demand for skills that complement and enhance these technologies grows. To thrive in an AI-driven world, students will need a robust combination of skills, ranging from technical know-how like data literacy and machine learning basics to soft skills such as critical thinking and emotional intelligence.

Essential AI Skills

One fundamental skill to have in an AI-driven landscape would be data literacy. It involves understanding how data is collected, analyzed, and utilized to make decisions. By becoming data literate, students learn to critically analyze information in an age where data is ubiquitous, which is crucial for navigating the digital world responsibly and effectively. Additionally, a basic understanding of Machine Learning processes—the backbone of most AI systems—equips students with insights into how algorithms learn from data to make predictions or perform tasks. This knowledge demystifies AI technologies and prepares students for more advanced studies or careers in tech-driven fields.

Ethical computing is another critical area that needs emphasis. This is all about understanding the moral implications of technology and AI, such as privacy concerns, bias in algorithmic decision-making, and the broader societal impacts of automation.

Educating students on these topics encourages the responsible use and development of AI technologies, ensuring they contribute positively to society.

Integrating Soft Skills

While technical proficiency is crucial, it cannot ever replace soft skills, which remain indispensable in an AI-driven world. Critical thinking, for instance, allows students to effectively analyze and evaluate information from various sources to make reasoned decisions. This skill is increasingly important as AI systems present us with complex data and choices. Problem-solving skills enable students to navigate challenges and find effective solutions, a valuable ability in academic settings and the workplace.

Adaptability is another key skill, especially in an environment continually reshaped by technological advancements. Adaptable students can navigate changes more effectively and are better prepared to learn new technologies as they emerge. This skill ensures that students are not just prepared for the world as it is but for the myriad changes the future may bring.

Learning Strategies

Integrating skills like the ones I just mentioned into the curriculum requires innovative teaching strategies that engage students in meaningful learning experiences. Interdisciplinary approaches, where students apply AI and data literacy skills across various subjects—from science to humanities—help students see the relevance of what they learn in real-world contexts. Project-based learning, in which students undertake projects that require the application of multiple skills to solve complex problems, can be particularly effective.

These projects enhance learning and prepare students for the collaborative, multifaceted nature of most modern workplaces. For example, a project could involve students creating a simple machine-learning model to analyze historical weather data and predict future weather patterns. Such a project would improve their understanding of Machine Learning and enhance their data literacy and problem-solving skills. Moreover, discussing the implications of their findings on real-world issues like farming and urban planning integrates ethical computing and critical thinking into the learning process.

The Role of Emotional Intelligence

Emotional intelligence, the ability to understand and manage one's emotions and empathize with others, is particularly crucial in an AI-driven world. As AI technologies perform more cognitive tasks, the uniquely human skill of emotional intelligence becomes even more valuable than it already was in the first place. It plays a critical role in managing teams, making ethical decisions, and navigating the increasingly complex social and professional landscapes.

Nurturing emotional intelligence in students involves activities that require them to work in teams, resolve conflicts, and engage in community service. It also includes teaching practices that emphasize self-reflection, mindfulness, and empathy. These practices help students better understand themselves and others, fostering skills essential for personal and professional success in a technology-saturated future.

By focusing on these essential and soft skills and integrating them through dynamic and engaging educational strategies, you can prepare students not just to face the future but to shape it. This approach ensures that as AI capabilities grow, so too does your students' ability to use these technologies wisely, ethically, and effectively in ways that enhance both their lives and the broader society.

6.3 Bringing AI Literacy into the Curriculum

AI literacy, simply put, is the ability to understand and use AI technologies effectively and ethically. For students at varying educational levels, acquiring AI literacy means more than just learning to code or interact with AI systems—it involves understanding the implications of AI on society, recognizing the ethical considerations it entails, and being prepared to use AI responsibly in various aspects of life. As we weave AI literacy into educational curricula, it becomes crucial not only for fostering technically proficient graduates but also for ensuring these young minds can navigate and shape the digital world with informed ethics and critical awareness.

Developing curricula that incorporate AI literacy starts with identifying the critical components of what students need to know about AI. This includes basic concepts like algorithms and data models and more complex issues such as data privacy, bias in AI, and the societal impacts of automation and AI technologies. Educators must choose appropriate learning materials and tools that not only cover these topics but also engage students in a way that promotes deep understanding. For instance, interactive AI simulations that allow students to see the outcomes of different algorithms firsthand can be an effective learning tool. Additionally, assessment methods need to evolve beyond traditional tests and quizzes to include projects and presentations that allow students to demonstrate their understanding of AI in real-world contexts. Rather than merely being taught how to pass tests, students ought to be enabled to truly gain and retain knowledge.

Collaboration with technology experts and companies is vital in keeping the AI literacy curriculum current and practical. These partnerships can provide schools access to the latest AI technologies and learning platforms and offer students opportunities to engage with real-world AI applications. Tech companies can also assist in training educators to teach AI concepts effectively, ensuring they are familiar with the technology and confident in their ability to convey complex ideas clearly and accurately. Moreover, collaborations can open up internship and mentorship opportunities for students, providing them with invaluable industry experience and insights into potential career paths in AI.

To illustrate the successful integration of AI literacy into educational programs, I will share with you the story of a university that partnered with a leading AI technology firm to develop its curriculum. This collaboration resulted in a series of workshops where students could work alongside AI professionals on projects ranging from developing intelligent tutoring systems to creating ethical guidelines for AI use. The benefits of this integration were twofold: students gained hands-on experience with cutting-edge AI technologies, and they were also exposed to the ethical and societal considerations of AI, preparing them to be thoughtful, responsible users and developers of AI systems.

Another case worth noting involves a high school that introduced an AI literacy module into its computer science curriculum. The school developed the module in collaboration with an educational nonprofit specializing in AI education, which provided resources and training for teachers. Students in the program learned to design simple machine-learning models and were encouraged to consider the ethical dimensions of AI by examining case studies of AI in various industries. The challenge in this case was ensuring that the curriculum was accessible to all students, regardless of their prior experience with computer science. To address this, the school adopted a tiered approach to the module, with introductory lessons for beginners and more advanced projects for students with some background in coding. This flexible approach allowed all students to engage with AI at a level appropriate to their skills and interests, promoting inclusivity and ensuring that every student had the opportunity to develop AI literacy.

These examples underscore the practical steps schools and universities can take to integrate AI literacy into their curricula, highlighting the benefits of such integration for students' education and future career prospects. By developing thoughtfully designed AI literacy programs and collaborating with experts in the field, educational institutions can prepare students to traverse the complexities of an AI-driven world with confidence and critical insight.

6.4 The Role of AI in Career Guidance and Preparation

AI is transforming how educators teach and profoundly influencing career guidance and preparation. In order to prepare your students for a future intertwined with AI, understanding its role in career counseling is crucial. AI can analyze vast amounts of data regarding student performance, interests, and evolving market trends, providing personalized career advice that aligns with individual aspirations and job market realities. This tailored approach helps demystify the path to potential careers, allowing students to make informed decisions based on a comprehensive understanding of their strengths and opportunities.

Picture a system that can sift through data to identify a student's proficiency in areas like critical thinking or creative problem-solving and then cross-reference these skills with current and emerging career trends. Such AI-driven career counseling tools can highlight fields where these skills are in high demand, suggest educational paths, and even connect students with potential mentors and internships. These systems can also adapt to changes in the job market, ensuring that the guidance provided is up-to-date and reflects real opportunities. For instance, if there's a surge in demand for data analysts, the system could encourage students with strong analytical skills to explore this path, providing resources on relevant courses and workshops.

As the integration of AI across industries continues to grow, so too does the array of careers in AI and related fields. Preparing students for these opportunities means going beyond traditional computing skills. Educators must foster a deep understanding of AI concepts, ethical implications, and practical applications. This preparation involves equipping students with technical skills and ensuring they understand the broader context of AI integration in various sectors. By doing so, students can appreciate how AI works and how it can be applied ethically and effectively across different industries.

Furthermore, AI tools can play a significant role in enhancing job readiness among students. Platforms that assist with resume building and interview preparation can use AI to analyze job descriptions and recommend the most relevant skills and experiences to highlight. They can also offer personalized feedback on mock interviews, analyzing speech patterns, content, and delivery to help students improve their communication skills and confidence. These tools often use Natural Language Processing to provide feedback that is not only accurate but also contextually aware, ensuring that students receive advice that is genuinely beneficial and tailored to specific career paths.

While the potential benefits of using AI in career guidance and preparation are immense, it is essential to approach these technologies with a keen awareness of ethical considerations. If we don't, dystopian scenarios such as AI tools that are programmed to favor students of certain races over others will get awfully close to becoming a reality. Ensuring that AI-driven advice is unbiased and equitable involves constant vigilance and regular auditing of AI systems. Educators and career counselors must proactively identify potential biases in how AI tools analyze data and make recommendations. This might involve scrutinizing the algorithms for biases in gender, ethnicity, or socioeconomic background and making adjustments to ensure that all students receive fair and unbiased support. Additionally, transparency about how these AI systems work and how they make their recommendations is vital. Students should understand the mechanisms behind the AI advice they receive, fostering a sense of trust and allowing them to make more informed decisions about their educational and career paths.

In integrating AI into career guidance and preparation, you play a lead role in shaping how students perceive and interact with these technologies. By providing them with the tools and understanding necessary to make their way through an AI-driven job market, you not only enhance their readiness for future careers but also empower them to participate ethically and effectively in the broader dialogue about the role of AI in society. Your efforts in guiding students through this terrain are more crucial than ever, ensuring they are well-prepared to succeed in their careers and contribute to the evolving world around them in a meaningful fashion.

6.5 How AI Is Reshaping Continuing Education and Lifelong Learning

In the world of continuing education and lifelong learning, AI is playing a metamorphic role, redefining how adult learners engage with their educational pursuits. AI's adaptive nature is particularly suited to the varied and dynamic needs of adults who balance professional responsibilities with personal development goals. By personalizing learning experiences, AI caters to each learner's individual pace, style, and career aspirations, ensuring that education is not a one-size-fits-all model but a tailored journey that aligns with personal and professional growth.

AI's capability to create personalized learning paths is perhaps most evident in its ability to dissect complex learning data and generate insights that guide the learning process. For instance, AI systems can analyze past performance, preferred learning media, and pace to suggest customized learning modules. This means that a professional aiming to upskill in data analytics may receive a learning module that emphasizes visual learning techniques, interactive datasets, and real-time feedback, all paced according to their learning speed and time constraints. This personalized approach makes learning more effective by addressing individual strengths and weaknesses and enhances motivation by aligning learning activities closely with the learner's goals.

Furthermore, AI significantly impacts microlearning and upskilling, which are crucial in today's fast-paced, ever-changing professional environments. Microlearning, which involves short, focused learning segments designed for skill-specific upskilling, is particularly well-suited to AI integration. AI algorithms can curate microlearning content that targets specific skill gaps, allowing learners to acquire new competencies in concise, manageable segments that fit easily into their busy schedules. This method is efficient and highly effective, as it limits cognitive overload and allows for better retention of information. On the other hand, Upskilling benefits from AI's ability to predict industry trends and identify emerging skills. By analyzing job market data and current industry demands, AI can recommend upskilling opportunities that are most likely to benefit the learner's career trajectory, ensuring that the skills they acquire are relevant and marketable.

Accessibility is another critical area where AI is making significant inroads in continuing education. Traditional barriers such as geographic location, time constraints, and physical disabilities can often hinder access to this type of education. AI-powered platforms dismantle these barriers, providing flexible learning solutions that learners can access anywhere and anytime. For example, AI-driven platforms can offer speech-to-text features for learners with hearing impairments or adaptive user interfaces for those with visual impairments, making learning materials more accessible to a diverse range of learners. Moreover, the proliferation of online courses driven by AI ensures that quality education is not confined to physical classrooms but is available to anyone with an internet connection, expanding access to educational resources globally.

Predicting and adapting to the future learning needs of adult learners is one of the most groundbreaking aspects of AI in continuing education. Through predictive analytics, AI can forecast future career and industry trends, guiding learners toward courses and skills that will likely be in high demand.

By analyzing current job performance and ongoing professional development activities, AI can also identify potential career transitions and recommend specific educational paths that facilitate these transitions. This proactive approach prepares learners for future opportunities and helps them remain competitive and relevant in their careers.

AI's integration into continuing education promises to bring even more profound changes to how adults learn and develop professionally. The ongoing challenge for educators and developers is to ensure that these AI-driven learning environments remain inclusive, ethical, and focused on enhancing the human aspects of learning. By continuing to innovate and adapt, AI can provide lifelong learners with the tools they need to succeed and thrive in an increasingly complex and technology-driven world.

6.6 Preparing Teachers for an AI-Enhanced Educational Landscape

The readiness of teachers to integrate and utilize AI stands as a cornerstone for the successful adoption of these innovations in classrooms. The rapid advancement of AI technologies requires continuous professional development programs that equip educators with the foundational knowledge of AI and the pedagogical strategies optimized for an AI-enhanced learning environment. These programs are essential for keeping educators abreast of the latest AI tools and methodologies that can transform teaching and learning processes. By engaging in lifelong learning themselves, teachers can better foster a classroom atmosphere that values and utilizes constant knowledge growth.

Professional development in the context of AI in education extends beyond mere familiarity with new tools. It entails a deep understanding of how AI can be strategically integrated into lesson planning, student assessments, and classroom management. Educators need to acquire skills in interpreting data provided by AI systems to tailor instruction to meet the diverse needs of students. They also need to understand how to leverage AI for administrative tasks, which can streamline operations and free up more time for direct student engagement. Practical workshops and hands-on training sessions can be highly effective in this regard, providing teachers with real-world applications of AI tools and the confidence to implement them creatively in their teaching practices.

Moreover, the shift towards an AI-integrated educational environment should be embraced as a cultural shift within academic institutions. Leaders in education must champion a culture of innovation that not only welcomes the changes brought about by AI but also actively promotes experimentation and adaptation. Policies that encourage innovation in pedagogical approaches and a reasonable level of risk-taking can support this cultural shift, backed by administrative support and resources. By cultivating an environment that views technological change as an opportunity rather than a challenge, educational leaders can inspire teachers to explore new ways to enhance their teaching effectiveness with AI.

However, the integration of AI in education is not without its challenges. Many educators express concerns about the implications of AI, including the fear of being replaced by technology or the potential for AI to depersonalize the learning experience. These concerns are valid and need to be addressed thoughtfully. Open discussions and forums allowing teachers to express their fears and reservations about AI can help demystify AI technologies and clarify their role as supportive tools rather than replacements.

Training sessions focusing on the ethical use of AI and its role in augmenting the human aspects of teaching can alleviate fears and highlight the value of AI in enhancing educational outcomes.

Strategies to address teacher resistance also include providing clear evidence of the benefits of AI integration, such as case studies or pilot programs that demonstrate improved student learning outcomes and increased teacher satisfaction. Additionally, offering ongoing support and resources to teachers as they navigate the adoption of AI tools can build confidence and competence in using these technologies. Ensuring that teachers feel supported in their journey to integrate AI into their teaching practices is crucial for the successful and sustainable adoption of AI in education.

In sum, it is clear that the role of the teacher is not diminished but rather enriched by AI technologies. The effective use of AI in education relies on the skillful combination of human creativity and empathy with technological efficiency and personalization. By preparing teachers through comprehensive professional development, fostering a culture of innovation, and addressing concerns and resistance with empathy and support, we can ensure that educators are active participants in shaping the future of AI in education and equipped to use these technologies in transformative ways. This preparation is not just about adapting to inevitable changes; it is about empowering educators to lead the charge in creating more engaging, effective, and inclusive educational experiences.

Chapter 7
Overcoming Challenges and Addressing Concerns

I ntegrating AI into classrooms brings a shimmer of transformative potential coupled with a series of challenges and misconceptions. As educators and administrators, you are often at the frontline, dealing with these complexities, balancing innovation with practicality, and fostering an environment where technology enhances rather than eclipses the human touch in education. This chapter deeply addresses one of the most pervasive challenges: the fear and misconception surrounding AI as a potential replacement rather than a tool that augments and enhances the educational world.

7.1 Debunking the Fear: AI as a Tool, Not a Replacement

The narrative surrounding AI in education often veers towards the sensational—robots replacing teachers, algorithms dictating the future of our children—with such portrayals feeding into a deep-seated fear of a depersonalized education system where students are but numbers and technology reigns supreme. I find it of vital importance to debunk these myths once and for all and to underscore the true essence of AI as a facilitative tool designed to augment the educational process rather than replace the irreplaceable human educators at its core.

AI's role in education is akin to that of a sophisticated assistant whose primary function is to enhance the effectiveness of teaching and learning processes. For instance, consider the implementation of AI-driven analytics tools that assess students' learning patterns and identify areas where they struggle the most. Such tools provide you, the educator, with invaluable insights, allowing you to tailor your interactions with students more effectively. This personalized attention is not feasible at such a granular level without the aid of AI technologies, especially in larger classrooms where individual student monitoring can be challenging.

Moreover, the deployment of AI in routine administrative tasks—such as grading, attendance, and scheduling—is another area where AI proves to be a tool of empowerment. By automating these time-consuming tasks, AI frees up educators' time, allowing them to dedicate more energy to interactive and creative teaching. This shift enhances the quality of education and enriches the experience for both teachers and students, fostering a more engaged and responsive learning environment.

Acknowledging AI's limitations is as essential as recognizing its capabilities. By its current design and function, AI lacks emotional intelligence, moral reasoning, and the ability to make nuanced judgments—traits inherently human and critical in teaching. These limitations underscore the fact that AI is not here to replace teachers but to support them in ways that amplify their presence and effectiveness in the classroom.

By understanding these boundaries, educators can better integrate AI tools in a manner that complements their teaching methods rather than competes with them.

Promoting positive narratives about AI in education is essential if we seek to shift perceptions surrounding its role. Across the globe, there are myriad instances where AI has been successfully integrated into classrooms, not as a teacher replacement but as a powerful tool that supports educational goals. These success stories need to be highlighted and shared, illustrating the potential of AI to empower educators and enhance learning outcomes.

We ought to approach the use of AI technologies in education with a balanced perspective, understanding their role as enhancers rather than replacements. By focusing on the ways AI can augment the educational process and continually educating ourselves about its capabilities and limitations, we can harness its potential effectively and ethically, ensuring that AI serves as a bridge to a more enriched educational future.

7.2 The Financial Costs of AI Implementation

Incorporating AI into educational settings isn't just a technical decision; it's also a financial commitment. As you consider AI's possibilities, understanding how to manage and mitigate these financial implications is crucial. Let's explore some strategies that make AI implementation as cost-effective as possible, ensuring you can leverage these powerful tools without straining your institution's budget.

Exploring low-cost or even free AI tools can be a game-changer for schools and educational institutions looking to adopt AI without significant up-front investment. Many AI software developers offer basic versions of their products at no cost or provide educational discounts, allowing you to experiment with AI functionalities without committing substantial financial resources. These versions often include many core features necessary for academic purposes, such as data analytics tools for tracking student performance or AI-driven content customization platforms that adapt based on learner input. Starting with these options can help you assess the utility and effectiveness of AI tools in your teaching or administrative processes before scaling up to more comprehensive, premium solutions.

Furthermore, funding options for educational technology are rich and varied, encompassing a range of potential sources from governmental grants to private-sector partnerships. Many governments worldwide recognize the transformative potential of AI in education and offer grants specifically designed to facilitate technology integration in schools. These grants can provide the financial support necessary to adopt advanced AI systems, train staff in their use, and evaluate their impact on student learning outcomes. Additionally, partnerships with tech companies can offer mutual benefits; while schools gain access to cutting-edge AI tools and expertise, companies receive valuable feedback and data to refine their products. Engaging with local tech communities or reaching out to AI startups can open collaboration opportunities that include financial support or in-kind contributions to technology and training.

The long-term financial planning for AI integration is another critical element that requires attention. While the initial setup costs can be significant, AI systems, particularly those automating administrative tasks or enhancing resource management, can lead to substantial savings over time. For example, AI-driven platforms that automate grading and attendance can significantly reduce the hours teachers need to spend on these tasks, allowing them to dedicate more time to instructional activities, which can improve educational outcomes and, by extension, the institution's reputation and appeal. Moreover, AI analytics can help optimize resource allocation, ensuring that investments in materials, technology, and human resources are strategically based on data-driven insights about what contributes most effectively to student success.

In order to traverse these financial waters effectively, developing a detailed financial plan is essential. This plan should include a comprehensive cost-benefit analysis, considering the immediate costs of purchasing and implementing AI systems and the long-term savings and benefits. Such planning should also account for potential risks and variables, such as changes in technology standards or unforeseen maintenance costs. Tools like financial forecasting models can be invaluable here, helping you project the future economic impact of AI investments and ensure that these align with your institution's long-term educational goals and budget constraints.

By adopting a strategic approach to financial planning, seeking cost-effective AI solutions, and tapping into available funding sources, you can effectively manage the economic aspects of AI integration. This careful financial stewardship ensures that the benefits of AI in education are not overshadowed by fiscal burdens, allowing your institution to focus on what truly matters—enhancing educational outcomes through innovative technology.

7.3 Handling Technical Issues and Glitches with AI Tools

When integrating AI into educational environments, it's crucial to anticipate and prepare for potential technical challenges that may arise. These challenges can range from software compatibility issues to connectivity disruptions, each capable of impeding the effective use of AI tools in your classroom. Understanding these common technical hurdles and establishing robust support systems can significantly mitigate their impact, ensuring that technological glitches do not derail your educational goals.

Software compatibility problems often occur when AI tools are only partially compatible with an educational institution's existing hardware or software infrastructure. For instance, an AI-based learning platform might require a more recent browser version or more powerful processors than those available in your school's computers. These discrepancies can lead to functionality issues, where certain features of the AI tools do not operate as intended, or in worst cases, the complete inability to use the tool. Connectivity issues, another common challenge, can disrupt the smooth operation of cloud-based AI tools, which require a stable internet connection to function effectively. Intermittent connectivity can hinder the AI's ability to process data in real time, which is crucial for tools that adapt learning content based on student interactions.

Setting up dedicated technical support systems is essential to combat these technical challenges. This includes personnel, such as IT staff trained in troubleshooting and maintaining AI systems, and infrastructural resources, like server systems or dedicated computer labs optimized for running AI applications. Regular maintenance schedules should be a core component of these support systems, involving routine checks and updates to ensure that all hardware and software components function optimally. This proactive approach not only helps in quickly resolving any immediate technical issues but also in preventing many potential problems from arising.

Collaboration with AI tool vendors plays a significant role in maintaining the smooth operation of these technologies. Vendors typically offer support services that include regular updates and patches that fix known bugs and improve the functionality of their products. A solid relationship with these vendors ensures direct access to expert assistance whenever needed. This can be particularly valuable for addressing complex issues that require specific knowledge about the AI tool's inner workings. Regular vendor updates also ensure that your AI tools remain compatible with other technology systems in your institution, reducing the likelihood of compatibility issues.

Encouraging a community-based approach to troubleshooting can also be incredibly effective. By fostering communities of practice among educators who use AI tools, you create a platform for sharing knowledge and solutions related to common technical issues. These communities can function as a first line of support where educators can quickly find advice and workarounds from colleagues who may have encountered and resolved similar issues. This speeds up the problem-solving process and helps build a collective knowledge base that can benefit the entire institution. For instance, an online forum or regular meet-ups can be set up where educators share their experiences, tips, and tricks for handling specific AI tools. This fosters a collaborative environment that effectively enhances everyone's ability to integrate AI into their teaching practices.

By anticipating potential technical challenges, establishing robust support systems, collaborating closely with vendors, and promoting community-based solutions, you can ensure that the integration of AI into your educational practices is as smooth and effective as possible. These strategies help mitigate the impact of technical issues and enhance the overall resilience and efficiency of your educational technology ecosystem.

Remember: the goal is not just to adopt new technologies merely for the sake of adopting them but to integrate them in ways that enhance learning outcomes and support your educational mission.

7.4 Ensuring Equitable Access to AI Resources

In modern education, the integration of AI holds promise not only for enhancing learning outcomes but also for bridging gaps in educational equity. However, the benefits of AI can only be fully realized if all students have access to these technologies. Addressing the digital divide, therefore, becomes a critical step in ensuring that AI tools in education serve as equalizers rather than as new fronts for existing disparities. This issue touches on the core of educational equity, highlighting the need for strategic actions to ensure every student, irrespective of their socio-economic background or physical abilities, can benefit from AI advancements in learning environments.

The digital divide—the gap between those with easy access to computers and the internet and those without—is more than just a matter of technological access; it's a significant barrier to educational and economic opportunity. In many regions, particularly in underserved communities, students may not have access to high-speed internet or modern computing devices, essential for utilizing AI-based educational tools. This lack of access can severely limit the opportunities for these students to benefit from the personalized learning experiences that AI can provide. To combat this, schools and educational systems must advocate for and implement initiatives aimed at increasing technology access.

This could involve providing students with devices through loan programs, installing reliable Wi-Fi in schools and community centers, or partnering with local governments and organizations to offer subsidized or free internet access to low-income families.

Implementing inclusive practices is another crucial pillar in ensuring equitable access to AI resources. AI tools must be designed and utilized in ways that do not exclude students with disabilities. This includes ensuring that AI interfaces are compatible with assistive technologies like screen readers or speech-to-text programs. Additionally, educational AI content should be accessible in multiple formats to accommodate different learning needs and preferences. For instance, an AI tutoring system could be equipped with text-based and video-based interaction options to cater to various learning styles and needs. Training for educators is also essential, equipping them with the skills to use AI tools in ways that support all students, including those who might require more tailored approaches.

Advocacy for policies promoting equitable access to AI in education is vital. Educators, administrators, and policymakers must work together to push for legislation and policies that support the funding and infrastructure improvements necessary for wide-scale AI integration. This includes lobbying for increased investment in technology for schools, particularly those in underserved areas, and advocating for policies that support the development and deployment of accessible AI technologies. Such policies ensure that the deployment of AI tools in education adheres to principles of fairness and inclusivity, providing all students with the opportunities to benefit from these advanced learning tools.

Highlighting successful equitable implementations is a powerful tool for advocating broader AI integration in education. Consider a school district that implemented an AI-driven learning platform across all its schools, focusing on ensuring that every student had access to it both at school and at home. The district provided students with tablets pre-loaded with AI learning apps and arranged for low-cost home internet access for families without it. Teachers received training not only on how to use the AI tools but also on strategies for integrating these tools in ways that supported diverse learning needs. The result was a significant improvement in engagement and academic performance across the district, demonstrating that equitable access to AI can lead to substantial educational benefits. Sharing these kinds of case studies can inspire similar initiatives elsewhere, showcasing the potential of AI to support diverse educational needs and help close the gap in educational equity.

Undoubtedly, any approaches toward integrating AI into education must be thoughtful and inclusive, ensuring these powerful tools are accessible to all students. By addressing the digital divide, implementing inclusive practices, advocating for supportive policies, and highlighting successful implementations, we can harness the potential of AI to catalyze educational equity, opening up new avenues for all students to succeed and thrive in an ever more digital world.

7.5 Managing the Human-AI Relationship in Classrooms

As educators, fostering a healthy relationship between students, teachers, and AI tools is essential in maximizing the benefits of technology while maintaining a nurturing learning environment. Cultivating AI literacy stands as a foundational step in this process. By educating yourself and your students about AI—its functionalities, applications, and implications—you lay the groundwork for a classroom where technology is used thoughtfully and effectively. This education goes beyond just understanding how to operate AI systems; it involves delving into how AI decisions are made, the data they use, and the potential biases they carry. Such knowledge empowers you and your students to use AI tools more responsibly and creatively, ensuring these tools are servants to educational goals, not masters.

Ethical interactions with AI in the classroom are also of the utmost importance. This includes understanding and teaching the importance of data privacy, the need for consent before data is used, and the appropriate and fair use of AI tools. Embedding these principles into your classroom culture can be facilitated through regular discussions about the ethical dimensions of AI. For instance, you might hold a class session where students debate the use of AI in evaluating student assignments, discussing the benefits and potential pitfalls of removing the human element from grading. These discussions help students develop a nuanced understanding of AI ethics, preparing them to navigate the digital world more wisely.

Balancing AI and human interaction in your teaching practice is essential to ensure that the introduction of AI tools enriches the classroom experience rather than detracts from it. One effective strategy is to use AI for individualized learning tasks, where the technology's capabilities for personalization can be fully leveraged while reserving group projects and discussions for more human-centric teaching methods. This approach ensures that AI is used to enhance learning without replacing the valuable interpersonal interactions that are vital for student development. For example, an AI program might help students practice language skills or solve math problems at their own pace. At the same time, class time can be devoted to collaborative projects that build teamwork and communication skills.

Regular assessments of AI's emotional and social impact on students are also of the essence. These assessments help you identify whether AI tools support a positive learning environment or if they are causing stress or disconnection among students. Tools like surveys or feedback forms that probe students' feelings about AI interactions can provide insights into how these technologies affect their learning and social experiences. Adjustments can then be made to ensure that AI tools are used in ways that truly benefit students, supporting an atmosphere of inclusion and empathy. For instance, if students report feeling less engaged during lessons that heavily feature AI, it might be time to reassess how these tools are integrated into your teaching, perhaps by increasing interactive, human-led activities.

Addressing these considerations involves continuous learning, adaptation, and discussion to ensure that AI serves as a beneficial tool in the educational process. By fostering AI literacy, ensuring ethical interactions, balancing AI with human engagement, and monitoring AI's emotional and social impacts, you can create a classroom environment where technology truly enhances learning and development. This approach prepares students for a future where AI will be ubiquitous and ensures that their educational journey is rich and supportive, characterized by a thoughtful integration of human and artificial intelligence.

7.6 Advocating for Ethical AI: Empowering Educators to Lead the Way

I want to emphasize once again that the ethical implications of advancements in educational AI systems should not be downplayed. As educators, you are not only imparting knowledge but also shaping the ethical compass of future generations. Thus, positioning educators as ethical leaders in the integration of AI becomes nothing short of a critical endeavor. By fostering a deeper understanding and conscientious application of AI, educators can set standards for responsible use, ensuring that AI acts as a positive force within educational settings.

The development and implementation of ethical frameworks for AI in education are essential. These frameworks serve as guiding principles that align with educational institutions' core values and ethical standards. Creating such a framework involves a thorough understanding of the capabilities and potential risks associated with AI technologies. It requires a collaborative approach, engaging educators, administrators, ethicists, and technologists to contribute diverse perspectives. This comprehensive involvement ensures that the framework is robust, addressing a wide range of ethical issues from data privacy and security to fairness and transparency in AI-driven decisions. For example, an ethical framework might stipulate that AI technologies should enhance educational equity by providing personalized learning experiences tailored to the needs of all students without bias or discrimination.

Encouraging active participation by educators in AI governance is also vital. As I've pointed out, educators are on the front lines of technological integration in schools and have firsthand insights into how AI tools affect teaching and learning processes. Their involvement in decision-making processes helps ensure that policies and practices around AI use are technically sound, pedagogically effective, and ethically responsible. Active participation might consist of educators partaking in committees that evaluate AI tools before they are introduced into the classroom or making contributions to discussions about the school's AI strategy and policy development. This proactive engagement helps craft policies that are practical, reflective of on-ground realities, and aligned with the institution's educational mission.

Moreover, promoting ethical training programs is crucial in equipping educators with the necessary skills and knowledge to navigate the complex ethical side of AI. These training programs should cover a range of topics, including the technical aspects of how AI systems work, the ethical considerations of using AI in educational settings, and strategies for implementing AI responsibly. Additionally, these programs should encourage critical thinking about the broader impacts of AI on society and foster skills for ethical decision-making.

By understanding the intricacies of AI, educators can better anticipate potential ethical dilemmas and make informed decisions that uphold the integrity and values of their educational roles. For instance, a training session might simulate scenarios where educators must decide how to ethically use predictive analytics tools to support student success without compromising student privacy or autonomy.

The key takeaway of this chapter is the lead role educators play in steering the ethical use of AI within educational settings. In fostering a culture where educators are seen and see themselves as ethical leaders in AI integration, the educational environment can traverse the challenges posed by these advanced technologies more confidently and competently. By developing ethical frameworks, engaging actively in AI governance, and undergoing thorough training, educators can lead the way in ensuring that AI is used as a force for good in education, enhancing learning experiences while upholding fundamental ethical standards.

Let these principles guide your integration of AI, setting a standard of ethical excellence that not only impacts your classrooms but also extends to the broader educational community.

Chapter 8
Case Studies and Real-World Applications

I have extensively gone over the importance of sharing success stories of AI in education, for they serve as rock-solid evidence that successful and ethical integrations of these technologies in the classroom are certainly possible. I like to lead by example, and for this reason, I've shared multiple such stories with you already throughout the previous chapters. However, I decided that it was not enough, so I made the call to dedicate this last chapter to nothing but real-world examples of successful AI integrations in various educational settings to underscore in no uncertain terms my views and intentions one last time before you finish reading this book.

8.1 AI Success Stories: Transformative Impacts in Global Classrooms

Global Perspective on AI Integration

From Tokyo to Toronto, educators are turning to AI to enhance the teaching and learning experience. In Sweden, an AI language learning app has enabled immigrants to accelerate their Swedish language skills, fostering quicker integration into society. In rural India, AI-powered mobile classrooms provide children with personalized math lessons, many experiencing formal education for the first time. These stories underscore a common theme: AI's capacity to transcend geographical and socioeconomic barriers, offering tailored educational experiences that were once thought unattainable.

Diverse Educational Settings

The adaptability of AI comes to the forefront when you consider its application in both well-resourced and under-resourced schools. In Silicon Valley, schools equipped with cutting-edge technology use AI systems to analyze vast amounts of data on student learning patterns, enabling educators to fine-tune instructional strategies almost in real time. Contrast this with a school in sub-Saharan Africa where solar-powered AI devices offer literacy tools to children, many of whom have limited access to qualified teachers. These examples illustrate the versatility of AI solutions and their potential to democratize education, ensuring that every child, regardless of their circumstances, has the opportunity to learn and succeed.

Impact on Student Outcomes

The proof, as they say, is in the pudding. In a high school in South Korea, introducing AI-driven analytics to monitor student engagement and performance has led to a noticeable improvement in test scores, particularly in STEM subjects. Similarly, a middle school in the United States reported a significant increase in student participation and homework completion rates after integrating an AI homework helper that students could interact with via their smartphones. These improvements in student engagement and achievement are tangible indicators of AI's potential to elevate educational outcomes.

Teacher Adaptation and Innovation

As much as AI is a tool for students, it is also a catalyst for teacher innovation. Educators are harnessing AI to expand their teaching capabilities and redefine classroom management. A notable example is a teacher in Brazil who uses AI to track the progression of group projects, enabling real-time feedback and adjustments that keep students on track and engaged. Meanwhile, in Australia, teachers use AI-driven platforms to create dynamic, multimedia-rich lesson plans that adapt to the learning pace of the class, freeing up time to focus on creative and critical teaching moments.

◊ Interactive Element: Your Teaching Methods and AI

Consider how AI might change your teaching methods or educational environment. What potential benefits or challenges do you foresee in integrating AI into your classroom? Reflect on how these technologies could enhance or transform your approach to education.

Witnessing the transformative impacts of AI across our planet, it becomes evident that these technologies are not just tools of change but harbingers of a new era in education. Through these case studies, you are invited to see the potential of AI to not only support educational practices but to revolutionize them, ensuring every student has the chance to achieve their fullest potential.

8.2 AI in Higher Education: Case Studies of Campus-Wide Implementation

The landscape of higher education is witnessing a significant transformation as institutions across the globe integrate AI into every facet of their operations. This integration is not confined to isolated classrooms or specific departments; it encompasses entire campuses, creating ecosystems where AI enhances administrative and academic functions. Universities are deploying AI to streamline complex processes like admissions, student services, and personalized learning, fundamentally changing the way institutions operate and students learn.

Let's explore a university that implemented an AI system to revolutionize its admissions process. Traditionally, reviewing applications was both time-consuming and subject to human bias. The AI system introduced uses Natural Language Processing to analyze application essays, extracting insights about the applicants' creativity and critical thinking skills. Machine Learning algorithms assess historical admissions data to predict applicant success, ensuring a more data-driven, equitable decision-making process. This shift improved the efficiency and fairness of admissions and allowed admission officers to focus on strategic decision-making and personalized applicant engagement.

Furthermore, AI's role extends into enhancing student services and academic experiences. For example, AI-driven chatbots are deployed to provide 24/7 responses to student inquiries, from campus life questions to academic guidance. This instant, always-available support system improves student satisfaction and engagement, crucial factors in an institution's success. On the educational front, personalized learning AI systems analyze individual students' learning patterns and adapt instructional content in real-time, catering to different learning speeds and styles. This tailored approach helps students achieve better academic outcomes by providing them with resources and challenges matched to their unique needs.

Challenges and Resolutions in AI Implementations

However, integrating AI across a university campus is not without its challenges. One of the primary concerns is scalability—ensuring that AI solutions can be expanded and adapted to meet the needs of the entire student body and staff without loss of performance or quality. Additionally, ethical concerns, particularly regarding data privacy and the risk of bias in AI algorithms, are paramount. These challenges require thoughtful strategies and robust solutions to ensure AI's successful and ethical implementation.

Addressing the scalability issue involves significant upfront investment in infrastructure and a strategic approach to software development. For instance, when a leading tech university decided to implement an AI system to personalize learning for its 30,000 students, it first piloted the program with smaller student groups to gauge infrastructure needs and potential scalability problems. This phased approach allowed the university to address technical issues on a manageable scale and gather data to improve the system before a full rollout.

Ethical concerns are tackled by establishing strict data governance policies and involving ethicists in the AI development process. Universities are setting up committees to oversee AI implementations, ensuring that every AI application is reviewed for ethical implications. These committees evaluate AI algorithms for potential biases and monitor data usage to protect student privacy. By prioritizing ethical considerations, institutions comply with legal standards and build trust with their students and the wider academic community.

Evaluating the Long-term Impact of AI
on Higher Education

The long-term impacts of AI on higher education are profound. Institutions that have successfully integrated AI report improved operational efficiency and significant enhancements in educational outcomes. Students at these institutions benefit from highly personalized learning experiences and support services, leading to higher satisfaction rates and academic success. Moreover, the administrative staff enjoys reduced workloads and the ability to focus more on strategic tasks rather than routine processes.

For instance, a university that implemented an AI-driven advising system observed a notable increase in student retention and graduation rates. The system identifies students who may be at risk of dropping out and provides them with timely interventions, significantly improving outcomes. Another long-term benefit is accumulating large-scale data on student learning and behavior, which institutions continually use to refine their educational strategies and offerings.

These case studies underscore AI's transformative potential in reshaping higher education. By embracing AI, universities enhance their operational and academic capabilities and position themselves at the forefront of educational innovation, ready to meet the challenges of today's increasingly digital world. AI's role in higher education is set to expand, promising even more profound impacts on the way institutions operate and students learn.

8.3 K-12 Innovations: Practical AI Applications in Primary and Secondary Schools

In the vibrant world of K-12 education, AI is not just a futuristic concept but a present-day tool reshaping how foundational skills are taught and learned. Particularly in early education, AI's role is becoming increasingly prominent, offering innovative ways to enhance literacy and numeracy among young learners. One striking example is an AI-powered program that uses interactive storytelling to improve reading skills. This tool, used in several primary schools across the Midwest, animates stories as children read aloud, providing real-time feedback on pronunciation and fluency. The program adapts the complexity of vocabulary and sentence structures based on the child's progress, making reading an engaging and personalized experience.

Moreover, AI-driven math applications are helping students grasp basic concepts through gamified learning, where each correct answer leads to new levels or challenges, keeping students motivated and engaged. These tools make learning more enjoyable and allow for the tracking of individual progress, enabling teachers to identify areas where a student might need more support.

AI's impact extends significantly into special needs education, where personalized and adaptive learning environments are crucial. For instance, speech therapy apps powered by AI are proving to be invaluable resources. These apps, which are becoming increasingly common in schools across the globe, use voice recognition technology to help children with speech impediments improve their communication skills.

The software listens, analyzes, and provides feedback on speech patterns, helping to accelerate learning and build confidence in students who might otherwise require much more time to achieve the same results.

Additionally, AI-powered interactive learning environments are being used to engage students with autism, providing sensory experiences that can be adjusted to each student's comfort levels and learning preferences. These tailored environments help maintain focus and interest, which are often challenging areas for students with special needs.

Engaging underrepresented or underserved student populations is another area where AI makes a marked difference. Schools in low-income regions, where resources and specialist educators are often scarce, use AI to bridge the gap. In South Africa, for example, mobile AI labs are used to bring educational resources to underprivileged areas. These labs, equipped with AI-driven educational software, travel to different schools and provide students with lessons in STEM subjects. The AI systems track each student's progress and adapt lessons to cater to their specific learning needs, ensuring personalized attention many students would not otherwise receive. This helps level the educational playing field and inspires students from diverse backgrounds to explore and excel in STEM fields.

The value of continuous feedback from AI tools cannot be overstated, especially when it comes to refining teaching strategies and curriculum designs in K-12 settings. AI's ability to collect and analyze vast amounts of data on student learning behaviors and outcomes enables educators to make informed decisions about their teaching methods. For instance, a school district in California uses AI analytics to evaluate the effectiveness of different teaching strategies across its schools. The AI tools analyze student performance data and provide reports on which methods yield the best outcomes. This ongoing cycle of feedback and improvement has led to significant enhancements in curriculum design, more targeted teaching interventions, and, ultimately, improved student performance across the district.

From enhancing early education and supporting special needs students to engaging underserved populations and refining educational practices through continuous feedback, AI is not just supporting educational goals but is actively reshaping how education is perceived and delivered. This dynamic interplay between technology and education is a testament to the metamorphic power of AI, promising a future where learning is more accessible, personalized, and effective for all students, including the youngest ones.

8.4 AI in Nontraditional Learning Environments: Homeschooling and Online Education

In the realm of education, AI has cast a wide net, reaching into corners that traditional teaching methods often struggle to cover. Nowhere is this more evident than in non-trivial settings like homeschooling and online education, where AI has not just made a foray but has become integral to reshaping learning dynamics.

For homeschooling families, AI has opened doors to personalized educational experiences that were once the exclusive domain of well-resourced private institutions. AI-driven platforms can tailor coursework to suit individual learning speeds, styles, and preferences, ensuring that home-educated students receive a well-rounded and comprehensive education tailored just for them. Tools that adapt in real-time to a student's interactions provide immediate feedback and adjust difficulty levels, ensuring learners are neither under-challenged nor overwhelmed. Parents, often juggling multiple roles, find these intelligent systems invaluable as they can trust the technology to provide consistent educational value without constant supervision.

Transitioning to the broader landscape of online education, AI's influence is profound and game-changing, particularly in *Massive Open Online Courses (MOOCs)* and virtual classrooms with democratized access to education. Here, AI enhances interactions and engagement through sophisticated platforms capable of managing thousands of simultaneous learners. AI systems in these environments use data from student interactions to improve course content, personalize learning paths, and even identify when students might need additional support, significantly reducing dropout rates.

Furthermore, the shift toward AI-enhanced synchronous and asynchronous learning models in online platforms means that education is not only more accessible but also more engaging. For instance, AI-driven analytics help educators in MOOCs to understand learning patterns across diverse global audiences, allowing them to tailor content that resonates with cultural and educational nuances, thus fostering a more inclusive learning environment.

The support for remote learning, especially highlighted during worldwide challenges like the COVID-19 pandemic, underscores AI's role in ensuring continuity and quality in education. During the pandemic, schools and universities leveraged AI to quickly transition to virtual learning, minimizing disruptions and maintaining educational standards. AI-driven platforms were used to track student engagement and performance remotely, providing educators with critical insights needed to adapt teaching strategies to the new normal of remote education. These systems also enabled real-time communication and collaboration, key components that helped preserve the interactive essence of classroom learning. This swift adaptability maintained educational continuity during unprecedented times and highlighted AI's potential in crafting resilient educational systems capable of withstanding future disruptions.

For the independent learner, AI's capabilities act as a bridge to a world of self-directed education. Tools equipped with AI provide adaptive learning paths and self-assessment modules that encourage learners to take control of their educational journey. These tools often include features like personalized dashboards, where learners can track their progress, set goals, and receive recommendations on the next steps, whether it's deepening knowledge in a particular area or exploring a new subject. Additionally, AI-driven recommendation systems can suggest resources and connect learners with online communities, facilitating a richer learning experience. This level of customization and flexibility makes AI an invaluable ally for lifelong learners, continually adapting to their evolving educational needs and goals.

In these nontraditional environments, AI supports and enhances diverse educational models, making learning more personalized, accessible, and effective. It promises a future where education is continually adapted to meet the needs of every learner, regardless of location, background, or educational aspiration.

8.5 AI's Role in Educational Research and Development

AI is revolutionizing classrooms worldwide, as well as educational research and development, offering new methodologies for exploring complex educational phenomena and enhancing the development of educational products. One of the most significant contributions of AI in this arena is its ability to streamline the research process. Traditional educational research often involves laborious data collection, from distributing surveys to manually observing classroom interactions. AI technologies simplify these tasks through automated data collection methods, including digital surveys that synthesize and analyze responses in real time and observation software that can record and quantify classroom interactions without bias.

Moreover, AI excels in handling large data sets, which are increasingly common in educational research. Machine learning algorithms can swiftly analyze this data to identify patterns and trends that might take humans much longer to discern. This capability accelerates the research cycle and enhances the accuracy and reliability of research findings, providing researchers with robust insights into student behaviors, learning outcomes, and educational strategies.

AI has profoundly impacted the development of educational products. Take, for instance, the creation of adaptive textbooks, which adjust the content presented based on a student's mastery of the topic. These textbooks use AI algorithms to assess a student's responses to questions and tasks, dynamically altering the complexity of the content to suit the student's learning pace. This personalized approach helps maintain students' engagement and optimizes their learning experiences.

Additionally, interactive learning modules incorporating simulations and virtual environments that respond to student inputs are being developed using AI. These modules provide students with realistic scenarios in which they can apply their knowledge, receive feedback, and learn from interactive experiences.

The sophistication of these AI-driven modules allows for a more immersive and practical learning experience, catering to various learning styles and needs.

Collaborations between academia and tech companies are essential in pushing the boundaries of what AI can achieve in educational research and development. These partnerships leverage the strengths of both sectors: academic institutions contribute deep insights into pedagogical theories and methodologies, while tech companies offer expertise in AI development and scalability. For example, a major university might partner with a tech company to develop an AI system that can predict student success in STEM fields. The university provides research expertise and access to educational data, while the tech company develops the AI algorithms and ensures the system is scalable and user-friendly. These collaborations often result in innovative educational solutions that can be widely applied, benefiting a larger population of students and educators.

Looking forward, the potential research areas in AI and education are seemingly limitless. One emerging area involves exploring the ethical implications of AI in education, particularly how AI decisions are made and the impact of these decisions on students from diverse backgrounds. Researchers are beginning to use AI to study the fairness of educational algorithms, ensuring they do not (inadvertently) perpetuate biases or inequalities. Another research frontier is the development of AI systems capable of understanding and adapting to students' emotional and cognitive states, offering a more holistic approach to educational technology that considers both academic and emotional learning. This research is fascinating and essential in ensuring that AI technologies support all aspects of student development, preparing them for both academic success and personal well-being.

Integrating AI into educational research and development heralds a new era of innovation and understanding in education, offering a plethora of opportunities for mutually beneficial partnerships between tech companies and academic institutions. By leveraging AI's capabilities in data analysis, product development, and collaborative research, educators and researchers can enhance educational practices and outcomes, making learning a more personalized, engaging, and effective process. That said, I'm convinced that all this innovation will bring exciting possibilities and new challenges.

8.6 Bringing It All Together: Comprehensive AI Integration in a School District

In the heart of a dynamically evolving educational realm, a school district stands as a testament to the incredible capabilities of AI when implemented on a district-wide scale. This district, encompassing a diverse array of schools, from densely populated urban institutions to smaller rural establishments, embarked on an ambitious journey to weave AI seamlessly into every facet of its educational framework. The comprehensive AI strategy adopted was not merely about integrating technology into classrooms but about reshaping educational paradigms to enhance learning, teaching, and administrative efficiency across all its schools.

The scalability of the AI solutions implemented played a crucial role in the success of this district-wide strategy. Initially piloted in a select group of schools, AI tools such as personalized learning platforms and data analytics systems were gradually introduced to other schools in the district. Key to this phased rollout was the adaptability of the AI systems, which were designed to meet the varying infrastructure capabilities and educational needs of different schools. For instance, in more technologically advanced urban schools, AI was used to enhance sophisticated STEM programs, while in rural schools, the focus was on basic literacy and numeracy aids. This careful consideration ensured that the deployment of AI tools was scalable and sustainable, with ongoing support and updates provided to adapt to the ever-changing worlds of education and technology.

Stakeholder involvement was another cornerstone of the district's strategy, ensuring that the integration of AI was a collaborative and inclusive process. Educators, students, parents, and local community members were all engaged from the outset, contributing their insights and feedback through workshops, meetings, and feedback sessions. This inclusive approach not only facilitated a smoother adoption of the technology but also ensured that the AI solutions were attuned to the specific needs and expectations of the district's diverse community. Teachers were trained to use AI tools and integrate them into their pedagogy effectively, enhancing their teaching rather than overshadowing it. Students were introduced to AI through interactive sessions that demystified the technology and showcased its benefits in enhancing their learning experiences. Parents and community members were kept informed and involved through regular updates and demonstrations, highlighting the positive impacts of AI on student outcomes and school efficiency.

Assessing the impact of AI across the district revealed significant improvements in several key areas. Student engagement and academic performance saw notable enhancements, with personalized AI learning tools enabling more targeted support and challenges for individual students. Teachers reported greater efficiency in administrative tasks and more time available for direct student interaction, thanks to AI's automation of routine processes such as grading and attendance. What's more, the district-wide data collected through AI systems provided invaluable insights into overall educational strategies, identifying successful initiatives and areas needing improvement. However, the journey was not without its challenges. Issues such as data privacy concerns and the need for continuous professional development for teachers were addressed through ongoing training and strict data governance policies.

The lessons learned from this comprehensive integration of AI have been manifold. The importance of scalability and adaptability in AI solutions, the value of stakeholder involvement in the implementation process, and the transformative impact of AI on educational outcomes are just a few of the insights gained. These lessons continue to inform the district's approach as it adapts and expands its AI strategies, ensuring that the benefits of technology serve every student, teacher, and community member effectively.

It's clear that the journey of integrating AI into education is both complex and rewarding. The experiences of this school district provide a blueprint for others looking to embark on a similar path, highlighting the potential of AI to bring the performance of educational institutions across the globe to a whole new level.

Conclusion

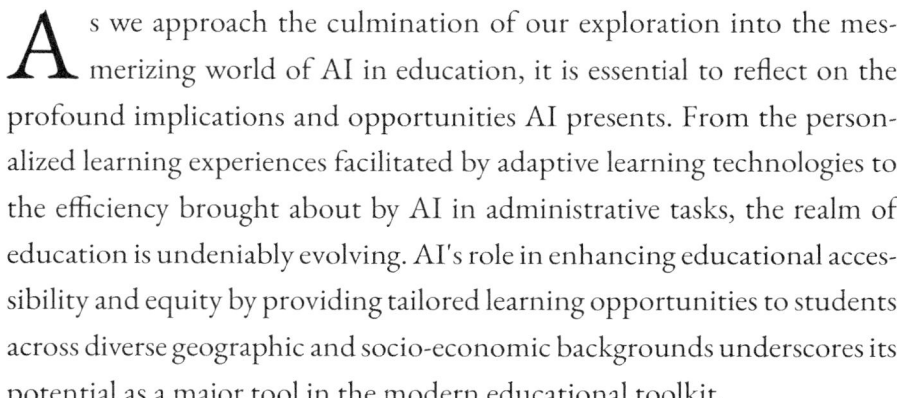

As we approach the culmination of our exploration into the mesmerizing world of AI in education, it is essential to reflect on the profound implications and opportunities AI presents. From the personalized learning experiences facilitated by adaptive learning technologies to the efficiency brought about by AI in administrative tasks, the realm of education is undeniably evolving. AI's role in enhancing educational accessibility and equity by providing tailored learning opportunities to students across diverse geographic and socio-economic backgrounds underscores its potential as a major tool in the modern educational toolkit.

However, as we harness these opportunities, we must navigate this terrain with a vigilant ethical compass. The importance of addressing data privacy concerns, mitigating biases inherent in algorithmic decisions, and ensuring equitable access to AI resources cannot be overstated. Educators and policymakers need to be aware that they form the first line of defense in ensuring that the integration of AI into educational settings upholds the highest standards of fairness and respect for individual rights.

At the heart of this technological revolution, the human element of education remains paramount. AI, despite all its capabilities, cannot replace the irreplaceable—the nuanced understanding, empathy, and interpersonal connections that educators bring to the learning environment. AI should be seen as a tool to augment and enhance these human qualities, not as a substitute.

Thus, I urge you, as educators, administrators, and policymakers, to proactively engage with the numerous possibilities brought to the table by AI. This engagement involves continuous learning and adaptation to keep abreast of technological advancements. It requires innovation in your professional practices to effectively integrate these tools in ways that enhance learning outcomes and operational efficiencies.

Collaboration will be key in this journey. The development and implementation of effective, ethical AI solutions in education must be a collaborative endeavor involving not just educators and policymakers but also tech developers and the broader community. Together, we can leverage diverse perspectives and expertise to create learning environments that are both innovative and inclusive.

The need for ongoing research and development in this field cannot be overlooked. Continued exploration into AI's educational applications and its impacts will drive evidence-based practices and policies, ensuring that AI contributes positively to educational outcomes. This research will also help understand and mitigate any unintended consequences of AI use in educational settings.

Looking ahead, the future of education augmented by AI appears promising and exciting. With AI, we have the potential to revolutionize educational paradigms, making learning more inclusive, personalized, and effective than it ever was before for students around the globe.

Let us embrace this future with optimism and a commitment to ensuring that technology serves to enhance, not undermine, the educational experiences that shape the leaders of tomorrow.

In closing, remember that the journey of integrating AI into education is continuous and dynamic. It presents challenges but also immense opportunities for growth and innovation. Let us move forward with resolve and enthusiasm, ready to transform these challenges into stepping stones for creating more engaging, effective, and equitable educational experiences.

Thank you for joining me on this enlightening journey, and may we all continue to strive for a future where every student has the tools and opportunities to succeed.

◊ Interactive Element: Your Turn

Using the QR code below, help people dedicated to education like you by posting a review of this book on Amazon. In this review, describe a way based on this book in which you would love to integrate AI into your classroom or academic institution and how this will bring your educational environment to the next level.

References

AnalyticVue. (n.d.). Predictive analytics in education: How can it help?
https://analyticvue.com/predictive-analytics-in-education/

Axon Park. (n.d.). How effective is AI in education? 10 case studies and examples.
https://axonpark.com/how-effective-is-ai-in-education-10-case-studies-and-examples/

Carter, J. (n.d.). Collaborative classrooms: How teachers and AI can work together. *LinkedIn*.
https://www.linkedin.com/pulse/collaborative-classrcoms-how-teachers-ai-can-work-together-carter-bkkje

Digital Promise. (2024, February 21). Revealing an AI literacy framework for learners and educators. *Digital Promise*.
https://digitalpromise.org/2024/02/21/revealing-an-ai-literacy-framework-for-learners-and-educators/

EdTech Magazine. (2020, January). Successful AI examples in higher education. *EdTech Magazine*.
https://edtechmagazine.com/higher/article/2020/01/successful-ai-examples-higher-education-can-inspire-our-future

eLearning Industry. (n.d.). AI and VR technology in education: The future of learning.
https://elearningindustry.com/evolving-education-the-impact-of-ai-and-vr-technology-on-the-future-of-learning

eLearning Industry. (n.d.). AR and VR in eLearning: Opportunities, challenges, and future possibilities.
https://elearningindustry.com/ar-vr-technologies-in-elearning-opportunities-challenges-and-future-possibilities

Elets News Network. (2023). Noteworthy AI trends in education and workforce for 2023. *Elets Online*.
https://wes.eletsonline.com/blog/noteworthy-ai-trends-in-education-and-workforce-for-2023/

European Commission. (n.d.). Ethical considerations in educational AI. *European Commission - School Education Gateway*.
https://school-education.ec.europa.eu/en/insights/news/ethical-considerations-educational-ai#:~:text=The%20integration%20of%20artificial%20intelligence,must%20function%20as%20guiding%20principles.

Every Learner Everywhere. (n.d.). 7 adaptive learning case studies that show when and how it is effective.
https://www.everylearnereverywhere.org/blog/7-adaptive-learning-case-studies-that-show-when-and-how-it-is-effective/

Georgetown University Center for Security and Emerging Technology. (n.d.). AI education in China and the United States. https://cset.georgetown.edu/publication/ai-education-in-china-and-the -united-states/

Gowers, T., & Parameswaran, K. (2020). Algorithmic bias detection and mitigation: Best practices and policies to reduce consumer harms. *Brookings*. https://www.brookings.edu/articles/algorithmic-bias-detection-and-mi tigation-best-practices-and-policies-to-reduce-consumer-harms/

IEEE. (2019). Ethically aligned design: A vision for prioritizing human well-being with artificial intelligence and autonomous systems (Version 2). https://standards.ieee.org/wp-content/uploads/import/documents/oth er/ead_v2.pdf

India Today. (2024, March 21). Rural education revolution: How AI reaches every corner of learning. *India Today*. https://www.indiatoday.in/education-today/featurephilia/story/how-ai -is-revolutionising-rural-learning-ai-in-technology-personalised-learning -2517592-2024-03-21

International Baccalaureate Organization (IBO). (n.d.). Artificial intelli- gence (AI) in learning, teaching, and assessment. https://www.ibo.org/programmes/artificial-intelligence-ai-in-learning-t eaching-and-assessment/

International Society for Technology in Education (ISTE). (n.d.). Arti- ficial intelligence explorations for educators. https://iste.org/courses/artificial-intelligence-explorations-for-educators

iTransition. (n.d.). AI in education: 8 use cases, real-life examples & bene-fits.
https://www.itransition.com/ai/education

Johnson, W. L., Rickel, J. W., & Lester, J. C. (2000). Artificial intelligence in education: Addressing ethical concerns. *Proceedings of the IEEE, 88*(8), 1304-1315.
https://www.ncbi.nlm.nih.gov/pmc/articles/PMC8455229/

Lester, J. C., & McLaren, B. M. (1994). Intelligent tutoring systems: An overview. *AI Magazine.*
https://www.aaai.org/Magazine/magazine-contents-1994.php

Marr, B. (2024, February 9). How generative AI will change the jobs of teachers. *Forbes.*
https://www.forbes.com/sites/bernardmarr/2024/02/09/how-generative-ai-will-change-the-jobs-of-teachers/

Massachusetts Institute of Technology Integrated Learning Initiative. (n.d.). Evaluating the effectiveness of AI-generated personalized learning content: Improving engagement.
https://mitili.mit.edu/research/evaluating-effectiveness-ai-generated-personalized-learning-content-improving-engagement

Molnar, A. (1997). Computers in education: A brief history.
University of Illinois.

New America. (n.d.). Artificial intelligence in schools: Privacy and security considerations.
http://newamerica.org/oti/blog/artificial-intelligence-in-schools-privacy-and-security-considerations/

OpenAI. (n.d.). Documentation and updates from OpenAI on ChatGPT and its development. *OpenAI News*.
https://openai.com/news/

OpenAI. (n.d.). OpenAI's description of GPT models and their capabilities. *OpenAI Platform*.
https://platform.openai.com/docs/models

Spector, J. M. (2001). History and trends of educational technology. *Educational Technology, 41*(1), 17-28.

TeacherMade. (2023). 10 of the best AI tools for teachers in 2023. *TeacherMade*.
https://teachermade.com/10-of-the-best-ai-tools-for-teachers-in-2023/

Thinkful. (n.d.). AI and education: Personalized learning and adaptive curriculum.
https://www.thinkful.com/blog/ai-and-education-personalized-learning-and-adaptive-curriculum/

University of San Diego. (n.d.). 43 examples of artificial intelligence in education. *OnlineDegrees*.
https://onlinedegrees.sandiego.edu/artificial-intelligence-education/

U.S. Department of Education. (n.d.). Artificial intelligence and the future of teaching and learning.
https://www2.ed.gov/documents/ai-report/ai-report.pdf

VKTR. (n.d.). 5 AI case studies in education.
https://www.vktr.com/ai-disruption/5-ai-case-studies-in-education/

Printed in Great Britain
by Amazon

61099749R00087